To Ellie &
Bill wonderful.
hostess in Minnesota.

God bless you.

Ari

Moral Rearmament.
January 5th. 2000

Wulf Kahan

my
FATHER

Compilation by Ari Kahan

Translation by Sandra Bessudo

Edition coordinated by SEPROSE, S.C.
ISBN 970-91375-2-2
Wulf Kahan, my Father
Ari Kahan Freund
Miguel de Cervantes Saavedra No. 376
Col. Irrigación 11500, México, D.F.

Translation by Sandra Bessudo, from the original book
Wulf Kahan, mi Padre.
Fourth edition in Spanish, 1994.
This edition is published by Imprebal.
First edition in English, 1996
Second edition in English, April, 1998.

Printed and bound in México.

Index

To Zev Ben Saul

Note from the author

In order to avoid any confusion, I would like to mention that the names Wulf and Adolfo will be used indistinctly to refer to the main character in this book. When he first arrived in Mexico, the boys in the neighborhood couldn't pronounce the name Wulf, so they thought it better to call him Adolfo; for such reason, I tried to respect the name that each person interviewed wanted to use for "Wulf-Adolfo" Kahan.

I deeply thank all the people who donated their time for an interview or collaborated in sending manuscripts. And along with my gratitude I would like to apologize for not being able to include every word, every idea, every contribution: the material obtained surpassed by far all publishing possibilities.

Although some of this material wasn't published, we appreciate it no less; on the contrary, we thank all the anonymous authors that also made this book possible!

Finally, one always ends up talking about that which one loves; I hope, in this case, I haven't talked too much.

PROLOGUE

Death can put an end to life, but never will it end a relationship.

I thought I knew my father, Wulf Kahan, pretty well, but having new information of who he was and having it heard from others makes me know him better. It gives me the chance to discover sides of him I ignored, aspects of his life that perhaps I suspected, and now, like a reflection on a mirror, they become a fascinating revelation.

Contemplating my father's figure through someone else's eyes has helped me, has given me the capability to tell others who he was, to converse with him out loud, as I've always done in my heart.

As a result of his death, I have read a lot about parenthood. I would humbly like to share some opinions regarding this topic. I'm not trying to make myself out to be an authority on this matter, nor to propound complex theories on the relationship between parent and child. Neither am I attempting to write an elegy on Wulf Kahan. My only intention is to talk about him, tell what others have told me. I want to narrate the life of a simple man, the life of a father like many, but who for me was special: talk about Wulf Kahan is all I intend to do.

I have found that I wrote this book because it lets me take a place in a certain historical moment in the chain of generations, where I received my father's teachings and now, it's time for me to enrich my role as a parent before my children, who are already parents as well.

Being among our parents, who we ought to outlive, and our children, who will outlive us, gives our life a very special meaning. Parenthood enriches the experience of life and, besides, it allows us to merge with the past and project ourselves into the future.

The relationship between a father and his son is established on competition; on the other hand, the bond between grandfather and grandson lets us experience the freedom of sharing precious moments of our life with a grown man and remain anchored to the certainty of the family bonds and origins. It is said that our grandparents are a reflection of the past and our children a vision of the future. Therefore, another reason why there is no competition among a grandfather and his grandson is that they are going through different situations: one is enjoying his golden years, the other, is just taking his first steps on the road of life.

Wulf Kahan was also a grandfather and when I asked one of his grandchildren what had been the most important thing that his father had given him he answered, "My granddad." I then asked what had he learnt from him and he said, "first of all, discipline; second, I learned a lot from his wisdom; and third, the importance of knowing your roots."

Some cultures believed that when father and son lived together, were both tolerant enough, spent numerous hours working together, going through challenges and mistakes, learning from each other, a substance, just as if it were some kind of food, passed from the older body to the young one. It was also said that the proper way to raise a child was through examples, for noble teachings and a heart that's sincere is a child's best learning source.

It is so much what I learned from Wulf Kahan...so many times he pulled me away from my fears with not a single word, just examples. I think I truly found a friend in him, the best friend ever. He'd always listen to me patiently and then, he would say what was on his mind but always gave me the opportunity to go ahead with whatever I had decided. If he thought me wrong, he'd try to convince me but would finally give up and step aside. In short, he let me grow.

What I most admired about Wulf Kahan was his perseverance. His presence, his existence, was what I enjoyed the best. And ours became such a full father and son relationship thanks to my mother, Estela Kahan, whose respect, admiration and love for my father was passed on to me. I always picture them side by side: quietly, my mother would listen, rather than just hear him speak, letting her relationship with my father develop in the best possible way, stepping aside when necessary, smoothing disputes, building the foundations of a relationship that would surpass their own deaths.

My father became ill and stayed that way for two years; and, as his final days grew nearer, I wished more than ever to be closer to him, to his thoughts, to his limitations, and to his love. The three days prior to his death we spent the most loving moments together, not knowing that those would be the last. He wanted to die, he wanted to rest, and when it finally happened, I felt that he had liberated himself from his body, that he had achieved absolute freedom.

Wulf Kahan and his elementary school classmates and teachers in Vilno (Poland).

CHAPTER I

The Immigrant

I wish not to be a common man, I have the right to be outstanding, if I can.

I seek opportunity, not certainty.

I wish to take risks deliberately.

Build failures and find success.

I refuse to give up my dreams for pension money.

I prefer the challenges of life, rather than a guaranteed existence.

The emotions of achievement, rather than the tranquillity of Utopia.

My heritage is the right to think and act on my own.

To enjoy the benefits of my actions, to look at the world face to face and say, "this is my creation".

D. Alfanza

"Wulf Kahan told me that he had come here as a child from Russia in a very precarious economical situation and had lived in Mexico since. He dedicated his whole life to hard work and therefore he was able to make a good patrimony", *narrates Christian Schjetnan.*

"I remember Wulf liked to talk about his roots, and so, I've thought that a book could be written about a Jewish immigrant and how he starts selling used car parts. This way, the following generations could realize how those people, empty-handed, started a life of hard work; no time or money wasted. They haven't done it only for themselves, they've also ensured a good life for two generations to come, their children and grandchildren."

"I believe Wulf Kahan to be a marvelous example of what Mexico has offered to the people that have come from their countries of origin, immigrants that arrived with no knowledge of the language, no money, nothing. The story is worth writing."

This book is not exactly a story, but a biographical profile, a collection of anecdotes, opinions, and descriptions given to me by many people that, for one reason or another, knew Wulf Kahan. Such is the case of writer Salo Grabinski, who says: "Mr. Szewel Kahan, originally from Russia, decided in 1926 that life in the Soviet Union was far too dangerous. There were persecutions and economical and political problems so, along with his wife Ana and children, he decided to leave the country."

"But Mr. Szewel had been trained as a flour mill technician and the Soviet authorities would not let him out of the country. This left him no option but to divorce his wife so she and his children could leave to Vilno[1], in Lithuania. Later, Mr. Kahan crossed the border gates and escaped Russia to reunite with his family."

"Then, alone, he immigrated to the American continent in search for fortune. Some time later, his family arrived in Veracruz where they were met by Szewel and, all together again, they traveled to Puebla. There, they moved into a small apartment in which they built an oven to bake European style bread so they wouldn't feel that much of a change. They had to wait for their documents to go to the United States where they had relatives; therefore, the family planned on staying in Puebla not for long. It was here where Mr. Kahan earned his first 200 Mexican pesos: it turned out that he found a broken down steam flour mill and asked the owner for that amount if he could manage to make it work again, and so he did. Ever since, we can catch a glimpse of the Kahan's interest in machinery."

"My mother, Ana, came from Poland and Szewel, my father, from Mogilov, Russia," *says Luis Kahan, Wulf's younger brother.* "Adolfo and I were born in Vilno, Lithuania. We used to live there; we came here on a ship, and traveled on third class for about thirty days. I remember a few details

[1] *A traditional town, once called "Lithuania's Jerusalem", where roads crossed and cultures came together. It went through times of persecution an destruction, but always survived; a place of philanthropy and tradition.*

about our trip at sea: in fact, sometimes we could go out on deck, but mostly we spent our time piled up inside. Adolfo himself remembered our arrival in Cuba: we didn't leave the ship, we had no money, and we fed from the fruit the Cubans threw on board as a welcoming to the immigrants. We were amazed at the delicious aroma of the mangos and bananas, fruit unknown to us until then."

"Of all my brothers, Salomón was the oldest, then came Adolfo, and then myself, Luis. Our birthdates are determined by the Jewish religion's system. They fall on certain days according to the setup of traditions and holidays."

"Adolfo was born on Kol-Nidre, Yom Kippur's eve. I decided to choose an important date as a birthdate, one that wasn't easy to forget: October 12. Adolfo, who was about nine years older than me, liked that date a lot so he chose October 13 as his birthdate. We practically had our birthday celebrations at the same time. Whenever we had a birthday party, what we did was celebrate together. This was more than just a birthdate to me; I considered Adolfo to be my second father. He was, as a matter of fact, the one who interceded between my father and I."

"We left escaping from the persecutions," *Luis remembers,* "we arrived here in 1926, somewhere around March, after we had lost two sisters: one in Mogilov, due to encephalitis caused by an apple that had hit her on the head at the age of eight, or so they said; the other one died of measles when she was three. My mother, my two brothers, and myself traveled here on our own because my father had immigrated first. He was a mill engineer and had worked for about a year in Puebla where he first lived right after arriving from Russia."

"We then moved to Mexico City; there were not many flour mills here; all the wheat was brought from Puebla where the flour industry was quite important. They sent wheat to cities all over the country. My father worked for Mr. Marcelino Presno and Mr. Perkins building baker's ovens and flour mills. He also had a job repairing railroad engines."

"Adolfo was the first to get married, even before Salomón did. By then we already had a car repair shop, called *La Europea*, on Balderas and Colon Street, No. 27; that's where we started off. We lived next door, in a modest neighborhood apartment building. It had a very spacious patio, some kind of a garage, and a man there whose last name was Dorado rented the garage located on 23 Mina Street. It was then that my father, a mechanic, took it into his head to disassemble used cars. And in that space, in a corner, he would take them apart and sell the pieces as spare parts."

I'll give the floor now to Wulf Kahan himself who, from his memoirs, will continue narrating his story:

"In 1926, my father and I started a used car parts business with a budget of 200.00 pesos, which in those days was a lot of money; we were very enthusiastic and dedicated. Sometimes we worked up to eighteen hours a day, including Saturdays and Sundays. Fortunately, it didn't take us long to get credit from some car and truck dealerships that were just starting out then. I still remember that I'd go with my father to buy some vehicles and, when the price was agreed on, my father would tell the salesman:

'I'll take these, but I don't have any money'.
The dealerships asked:
'How will you pay us?'
'I'll pay you when I sell the cars'.

"Then, only having to sign nothing other than the cars' sign out papers, they trustingly gave my father the vehicles. That's how we started selling used cars and trucks. Within a few years, by the early thirties, we started importing new vehicles. We brought them from the boarder on trailers; some, on ship containers arrived in Veracruz; and some others, were brought to Mexico City by train. That's when I first realized the importance of being honest and keeping one's word. My father always used to tell me: «it's better to have credit than a pocketful of money.»"

Luis Kahan continues:
"We moved to 23 Mina Street where the *Guadalupe* garage was; there, they had, and still have a very large image of the Virgin of Guadalupe in front of which the people used to cross themselves and throw coins as a gift. Someone from a church nearby would come and take all the coins. In those days, the differences between Jews and Catholics were pretty marked; nevertheless, although we weren't Catholic, we took good care of that altar because it was right on the entrance of our garage and there would always be some boy who would try to steal the money."

"Our janitor, *El Charrito*, couldn't read or write but he would jealously watch over the Virgin's money. I still remember our telephone number: 274-75. *El Charrito* never answered it because he was afraid of it, he was scared to death of it. There was a tiny office at the entrance and we lived further inside the building. That was on 23 Mina Street, where we disassembled cars; and we also had a place on Juárez Avenue No. 110. I would go to school in the mornings and during the afternoons I would help my brothers and my father in taking cars apart. I remember we truly were very poor; we barely had enough to survive with."

"I remember it as if it was yesterday...there was a huge patio, with a beautiful fig tree and around it were the bedrooms and the dining room. I didn't have a bedroom of my own: one was my brothers' bedroom, another, we rented out to some friends of ours, and the third was my parents'; I slept on some kind of couch in the dining room."

"We had no money; if I received a five or ten cent allowance it was too much. When there were figs on the tree I would pick them all, wrap them in a bed sheet, and go out to sell them. My brothers weren't into that kind of things but I had friends who helped me out. If I saw someone coming, I would pick the sheet up and run after him. That way I earned some money, which I invested in those thick comic books I liked so much: I remember their name was *Leoplan*, an Argentinean comic book filled with adventures and interesting facts. My mother was a saint, she used to defend us from our father's strong nature. He didn't like it when I did those kinds of deals."

"During the time we lived there, my dad was very fond of dogs; my mother had a very hard time when preparing food for them. We had dogs of all shapes and sizes, mostly streeters; there was a time we had up to fifteen dogs living with us. All of us at home respected my father's love for animals."

"My mother, Ana, always looked after the family finances. She used to go to the repair shop everyday and take care of the clients. She never missed a day until she felt the business was well under way. Her housework wasn't easy either, having to cook, clean, do the laundry, and prepare food for so many dogs. Once she saw things were going well in my father's shop, she dedicated herself to helping other people in need, but especially, you could say she was an excellent '*shatchente*'[2]; it hurt her to see a young girl not get married. If she saw a poor girl, young, single, she would collect the dowry and enough money among the people she knew to buy her the wedding dress and pay for the wedding expenses."

"Adolfo and I loved Mexican food; my parents didn't eat it as much although my dad did like hot peppers. My father did not eat pork, so my brothers and I would manage to sneak out to go eat pork meat tacos called *carnitas*."

Some of Wulf Kahan's friends also talk about those first years in Mexico; such is the case of engineer Isaac Grabinski, who says: "I know him since 1929, when he lived on Mina Street. They had a garage and his father,

[2] *Matchmaker*

Szewel Kahan, was just starting his business. I met him, his wife, and his three sons: Salomón, Adolfo, and Luis. Adolfo, who they called Wulf, was the one I was closest with, we were very, very good friends. We used to go to the YMHA (Young Men Hebrew Association) Club on 15 Tacuba Street. I was, along with other boys, one of the founders of the MACABI Club."

"We were both young; maybe 20 or 22 years old and, naturally, we would spend a lot of time together practicing sports and at social reunions. Adolfo was a man of a very special nature, he was a gentleman with the girls, the ladies, in every sense of the word. He would treat them very nicely."

"I was friends with him because we used to visit the same girls, like Estelita, who would later become Adolfo's wife. If we came home too late after a party, we would sleep out in one of the cars in the repair shop and, that way, no one at home would notice. Adolfo was one of the few boys who were well off in those days since he devoted himself to helping his dad in selling cars and had one of his own. Almost nobody did back then. I bought my first car from him in Puebla, but that was later."

"When we were young, we had a group of friends who respected and loved each other dearly; our wives had been friends since childhood, since the reunions at 15 Tacuba Street. Our families weren't in a good economical situation, some didn't live well at all. Therefore, the girls couldn't buy too many dresses for themselves and we couldn't invite them out very often. The idea of having reunions came from

From left to right: Isaac Grabinski, Moisés Derzavich, Wulf Kahan, Samuel Dultzin, Nathán Grabinski, Carlos Fishbein, and person not identified.

our desire to meet girls, but almost none of us could pick them up in a car. That's why we would go to the MACABI Club to spend some time with them. Years later, many of us, who had already become friends at the Club, founded the Centro Deportivo Israelita de Mexico (Mexican Jewish Sports Center)."

One of the girls Mr. Grabinski was referring to was Estela Freund, who later became Wulf Kahan's wife. She remembers that when Wulf was courting her, people would tell her:

'Estelita, don't tell me that you're going to marry that boy! Look how he dresses, always in that mechanic's overall. You deserve better'. *Paco Fernández would tell her. He was the antique dealer, owner of* 'La Granja', *the antique shop next door to her father's jewelry,* 'Joyería Amigo'.

She comments about those times: "my dad was a jeweler. My mother and us, her four children, came to Mexico with him. The fifth child was already born here. More immigrants came during that time and my parents met the Kahan's. Both couples started getting together on Sundays and Adolfo wouldn't even look at me then since I was too young. He was six years older than me, but I started growing, he started noticing me, and that is how he began courting me."

Mexico kept welcoming a large number of Jewish immigrants with open arms, letting them get involved in different activities, and giving their children the opportunity to get an education, to work and, well, to become a part of the country.

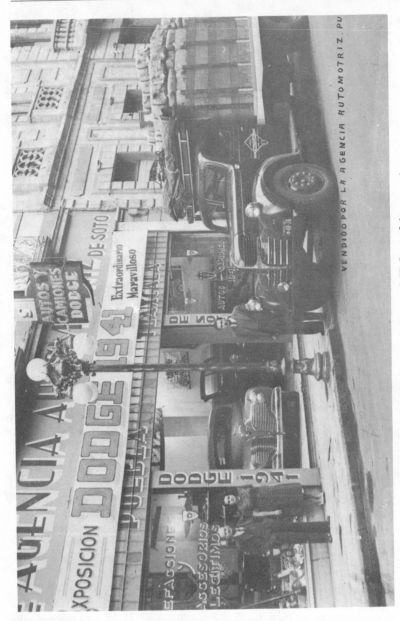

VENDIDO POR LA AGENCIA AUTOMOTRIZ, PU

At the dealership in Puebla: Szewel Kahan, his secretary,

CHAPTER II

Tough Times

Nowadays, the entrepreneur cannot use his talents exclusively in his own benefit; these are influenced by social purposes and become, in some way, part of the heritage of humanity.

> *Gastón Azcárraga Tamayo*
> *International Solidarity:*
> *A New Dimension*

Lecture presented by the Social Union of Mexican Entrepreneurs at the XII UNIPAC World Congress.

"In 1926," *according to personal notes written by Wulf Kahan,* "we opened an establishment on 27 Colón Street dedicated to buying and selling used cars and trucks, some of which were meant for being disassembled, and some renovated and resold. Ever since, we've had special preference for the Dodge line, due to its popularity among the used car consumers, to its solid body and frame, and to its powerful and durable four cylinder engine."

"That same year, we imported some Dodge automobiles from a distributor in Texas, which were brought by train to Mexico City and later sold to some clients in Real del Monte, in the state of Hidalgo. Previous to this, the cars went through the toughest quality tests, for it is well known that Real del Monte is a very mountainous area where silver mines are located; as there were a lot of narrow unpaved roads, the difficulties to get there were almost insurmountable: there were some parts of the terrain that had to be driven through on reverse gear. There were times the oil pan had to be greased with lard to keep the engine parts from melting together. You could say that those were the first cars to be driven in that part of the country. The vehicles were paid to us their weight in gold bars, a very peculiar currency in those times."

Luis Kahan goes on with the story telling about the frequent changes that came along in the family business:

"Adolfo was the one who helped my father the most. After the garage on 27 Colón Street, we opened up a repair shop called *Casa Kahan* on 110 Juárez Ave., just opposite to the *Caballito*[3], right where Bucareli Street and Juárez Ave. meet. We started selling new spare parts then and, at the same time, we kept on buying and selling used cars. Later on, we moved to a place located across the street from the 'Dos de Abril' market. The picture Adolfo had in his office was taken when we were still on Colón and Balderas."

The places on Colón Street and Mina Street were then used as storehouses and, according to Wulf Kahan's narration in this literary match with his younger brother, "we started importing more vehicles, especially new ones; they were mostly Chrysler cars, the Dodge line in particular. By then, we also started doing business with the authorized car dealers in the D.F.[4], the country's capital state, regarding the sale of used vehicles, a very tough market in Mexico City. We used to renovate the cars for resale in other parts of the country. It was back then that men in the same commercial field, like Mr. Rómulo O'Farril, Mr. Gastón Azcárraga V., Mr. Chase Crowley, and Mr. Pickard, helped us unconditionally, supplying us with car lots and letting us pay in long term installments."

"Later on," *Luis continues,* "we moved to the Hipódromo neighborhood. We lived on the third floor of a building on the corner of Insurgentes Ave. and San Luis Potosí. That's where we came up with the idea of moving to Puebla and opening up a branch of our repair shop and used car business. The

[3]   *A sculpture of a horse, well known in Mexico City and used as a landmark.*
[4]   *Initials for Federal District, Mexico's capital state.*

shop there was located on 531 Reforma Street. We would not go there all at once; sometimes someone stayed in Mexico City, usually Salomón, since he was still going to college, and the rest would go to Puebla."

"We built a loft in that shop so we could sleep over. It was terribly cold and we had a coal heater we used to turn on at night. When we started the business in Puebla, Wulf was already dating Estela and some time later, he wanted to get married. My dad was a difficult man to deal with when it came to marriages and he would put a lot of obstacles in the way; but finally, Wulf got married and lived here in Mexico City; not long after, came his first baby, Ari. Adolfo would travel to Puebla quite often, for he had to look after the shops in both cities."

Estela Freund herself tells us about those times:
"I was sixteen when I married Adolfo; my parents were against it at first because I had an older sister who was still single, and the same thing happened in his family. We both had to ask our older sisters for permission to get married. We dated for only eight months, which was very little time for those days. The wedding took place on June 21, 1936. We rented an apartment on the street of Campeche; that is how we started off our life together and Adolfo began to look for new ways of making money. I remember he had a $250.00 peso income per week and whenever he could, he would bring me a little present and then said: 'this is to make up for all I have not given you'."

Salomón, the oldest of the Kahan brothers, says that in those days "in which they had given us the Dodge dealership,

I was already working in my father's business, a few hours during the mornings and a few more in the afternoons, whenever I was not at school. I was studying hard to get my engineering degree and I found it very difficult to combine school and work. Adolfo was a very good brother; we would always be together and were very close; that is how it would always be, for better or for worse. He was a very sociable and whimsical person because he wanted us to have fun and would drag us to the parties after work."

Wulf Kahan continues saying that "during 1938, the year of the petroleum expropriation, we suffered a very severe economical crisis, for we owed a lot of money to other dealers that had given us credit. We had a high stock of vehicles, but we weren't selling, and had also stopped collecting payments due. We then called our creditors to ask for a reasonable term so we could cover our debts or, otherwise, hand them the keys to the business so that each one could collect what they were owed since the company's liabilities exceeded the assets. After many discussions, Mr. Case Crowley showed a gesture of great gentility: after hearing the balance and inventory report and listening to our proposal, he stood up and told the other creditors:

'Gentlemen, we must grant the Kahan's the terms they are asking us for to pay their debts; I shall answer for the total amount owed to us in case they don't fall due.'

That was the way our business was kept alive and that same year we opened another car dealership in the city of Puebla, on 531 Reforma Street, called *Agencia*

Parade float representing the Israelite Community of Puebla during the Independence Day Parade, on September 16, 1949.

Automotriz, S. de R.L.[5] Back then, another automobile company was offering us the distribution of their cars and trucks, starting with the 1938 models, but we put this offer on stand by for some time as to analyze the market potential for that make. Meanwhile, we kept on selling the high stock of vehicles we had back in Mexico City."

"The contract with the other company was practically ready to be signed when Mr. Raúl Azcárraga came to us and said that his brother, Mr. Gastón Azcárraga, wanted to talk to us regarding our business in Puebla, so we went over to his office on Reforma Ave., in Mexico City. It was then that we were offered the Dodge car and truck distribution for the states of Puebla, Tlaxcala, and part of Oaxaca, for he had just been given the Dodge and DeSoto vehicle assemblage and distribution franchise. Since Mr. Rómulo O'Farril had just given that franchise up, we were offered a minimum yearly quota of twenty-five vehicles; that way we didn't have to invest in getting larger facilities for the meantime; on the other hand, the other company was in fact demanding we get a bigger place. Having thought about the terms proposed to us and considering the special faith we had in Chrysler, based on former experiences, we immediately accepted their offer and set aside the one made by the other company."

"Ever since, we devoted ourselves to selling Chrysler products with all persistence, tenacity, and faith; we even exceeded our initial quota. One of our most outstanding

[5]   Limited-liability company *(Sociedad de Responsabilidad Limitada)*

moments, I remember, was the time we sold a Dodge truck to the *Cervecería Moctezuma* brewery branch in Puebla, whose manager then was Mr. Miranda; it was a high-priced truck and, for such reason, the plant would only take our order as long as we gave them a down payment. And we did, even though the brewery gave us no deposit. We brought the truck and it became so popular that later on the plant itself continued importing these vehicles. The same thing happened with a 28,000 pound tractor, which we first sold to *Hidalgo Hermanos*, in Puebla."

"At the same time that I was taking care of the business, I worried about my migratory situation. Before World War II started, I had begun to take the necessary steps in order to get my Mexican citizenship and it wasn't until December 1st, 1942 that I got my naturalization papers, which made me feel proud and safe to have a new homeland. I then started my military service, for now I had a land to defend."

"Due to the war, there was a shortage of vehicles in the marketplace and we found ourselves going through very critical moments; as a result of not being able to at least cover our expenses, we started importing used military vehicles directly from the United States, like the 4x4 and 6x6 Commando Dodge trucks and some passenger buses that were left over from the war. We drove them all the way to Puebla; that, of course, without giving up the Chrysler franchise we already had."

"When the war came to an end in 1945, we got the Dodge and DeSoto dealership as the Chrysler Corporation direct distributors for the city of Tampico, and created the *Compañía Automotriz del Golfo, S. de R.L.*"

"That was how, in 1946, we worked with both franchises, and each year we would aim to surpass our goals; therefore, we built facilities suitable for our activities, one in Tampico, on 91 Hidalgo Ave., and another in Puebla, on the corner of 17th Street North and Reforma Ave., No. 1703."

"As newlyweds," *Luis Kahan continues,* "my wife Raya and I moved to Tampico, back when we built the facilities on Hidalgo Ave. My brother Adolfo used to visit us quite often, but my dad stopped traveling that much then. Since I became ill with malaria, we decided to sell and go back to Puebla. My parents were living there with Salomón, who was already an engineer."

"In the year of 1949," *says Wulf Kahan,* "we moved back to Mexico City; we still owned the Dodge car and truck distribution franchise, so we established the *Compañía Impulsora Automotriz de México* dealership on the corner of Niño Perdido and Fray Servando Teresa de Mier."

"Back then, we would very often work almost 24 hours a day. The building was finished on January 18, 1952, one week ahead of the promised one-year period. Because of this, Mr. C.B. Thomas, Chrysler's Vice-President, had to fly all the way from Australia to keep his promise of personally inaugurating the building. It had a showroom with an area of 2,442 sq. ft. destined for new vehicles, a mezzanine floor with the same area meant for the Accounting Department offices, a 1,980 sq. ft. Used Vehicles

Department, and a 1,122 sq. ft. Maintenance Department, which totals an area of 7,986 sq. ft. with a different entrance for each department."

"The Board of Directors was formed as follows: President: Mr. Szewel Kahan; Secretary and General Manager: Mr. Wulf Kahan; Treasurer: Mr. Salomón Kahan; and Sales Manager: Mr. Luis Kahan."

"Among the best sales of that year was the one made to *Auto Transportes Los Galgos*, a transportation company which covered the Mexico-Acapulco route: thirteen Dodge vehicles with a seven passenger capacity each; we also sold ten vehicles of that same sort to *Auto Transportes de Lujo* covering the Mexico-Tampico route, as well as a fleet of trucks for furniture shipping to a moving company *called Muebles y Mudanzas, S.A.*[6]"

"Always aiming towards a constant sale increase and the achievement of a certain prestige for our products, we made it to 1954, year in which we suffered the effects of a currency devaluation and its consequences. Nevertheless, we managed to keep going and do well."

"On May 1st, 1955, we experienced the great sorrow of loosing the company's President and founder, and head of the family, Mr. Szewel Kahan. Despite this irreparable loss, the company had to go on with the same enthusiasm and persistence as before. It was then that the oldest in the family, Mr. Salomón Kahan, was named President of

[6]   *Corporation (Sociedad Anónima)*

the company; and Wulf Kahan became the Secretary, Treasurer, and General Manager. Then, in 1959, on the road to self-improvement, the company imported twenty Dodge Kingsway Sport Coupes from the United States."

"The year after, we bought a piece of land just opposite to where the company was located back then. It was on the corner of Fray Servando Teresa de Mier and Dr. Valenzuela, it had an area of 8,580 sq. ft., and was exclusively bought for selling our trucks."

"In 1959, another company was formed by the same shareholders; it was called *Automotriz Fran-Mex, S.A.* and had Wulf Kahan as President of the Board of Administration; as Secretary Treasurer was Mr. Salomón Kahan; Mr. Luis Kahan was the General Manager; and the position of Assistant Manager was held by Mr. Ari Kahan, the new addition to the family business, representing the third Kahan dynasty generation dedicated to the automotive field. This company would be in charge of selling the Simca automobile line."

"When *Automotriz Fran-Mex* was closed down in 1961, Mr. Ari Kahan became part of the head-staff at *Compañía Impulsora Automotriz de Mexico, S.A.*; by 1962, we managed to increase both our car and truck sales as we closed some deals with important enterprises such as Coca-Cola Mexico and a construction company called *Constructora El Aguila, S.A.*"

"By the end of that same year, our facilities went through some important changes: we built new offices for the company's executives and sales agents, new showrooms for new and used car exhibition, as well as a showroom destined exclusively for our used and new truck division. All this was done with the purpose of keeping up with the future plans in *Fábricas Automex, S.A.*'s industrial integration program."

At last, it looked like the tough times had passed, about which engineer Alberto Liz comments: "Wulf Kahan used to have, in a very special spot in his office, a photo of himself when young, standing beside his father behind the counter of a shop where they sold junk and old tools; nothing fancy, just a modest shop. I remember he had it for the longest time and was very fond of it; he had had it enlarged and proudly, he would show everyone how he had started out."

Mr. Federico Anaya also relates: "I met Wulf Kahan when my father, Gabriel Anaya, was Mr. Kahan Sr.'s lawyer, and later, worked for the three brothers: Wulf, Luis, and Salomón. Our relationship is one of the closest and oldest I know. Mr. Szewel Kahan met my father and, actually, I think he was one of the first persons he met here in Mexico. Wulf started out from zero and formed a tribal family."

Likewise, Dr. Miguel Angel Gil says: "Don[7] Adolfo would tell us about his family life; in the 30's, during the most difficult times, that businessman did something worth imitating: in spite of the country's unfavorable economical, political, and social situation, Don Adolfo achieved great growth in his enterprise. This is most important because,

[7] *Title of respect used before a man's first name.*

besides, immigrants were still not well accepted in Mexico in those times."

In 1965, the Kahan brothers decided to become partners with the Sprowls family. Two years later, the partnership was dissolved, which caused Wulf to suffer great depression for the Sprowls kept the business. He relates: "The support I received from my son Ari was very important because Luis, him, and I created a new company that would carry our family name along with all the responsibility that this implies. We were determined to continue in the car dealing business." *Again, he found himself facing another tough moment when he made the decision of opening a new car dealership on a leased property on 1056 Ejército Nacional Ave.*

"By the year 1975," *Wulf continues,* "our company had grown and *Kasa Automotriz* was founded, just opposite to *La Hacienda de los Morales* restaurant, and in which Samuel and Sergio Kahan, Luis' sons, and Jack, Wulf's youngest son, were participating already. When the devaluation struck in 1976, we had a very large debt in dollars and a very high inventory of vehicles, including 110 trucks. After a month with no sales whatsoever, every unit we sold would only represent money loss, for raising the new prices imposed on the cars was prohibited. A year later, the situation had not improved much so we decided to split the dealerships between the two families: Adolfo, Ari, and Jack kept *Kahan Automotriz*; and Luis, Samuel, and Sergio kept *Kasa Automotriz, S.A.*"

Tough times are meant for big challenges, and it was during those tough moments that Jack Kahan, with great effort, establishes a used car lot, Kar, S.A., *which would later become a Renault dealership. This franchise was sold to him by Mr. Harry Neuhaus, a businessman concerned about not leaving his workers among the unemployed when he died; that was the reason for which the sale of the company was conditioned by only one thing: no staff member working for the company could be fired. The dealership carried on with its activities until 1983, year in which Renault Mexico was retired from the market.*

In 1980, we had to turn to the Banco Internacional, *whose Director then was Mr. Manuel Sánchez Lugo, for credit to buy some land, for the owners of the property we were leasing at the time on Ejército Nacional did not want to renew our contract.*

The land Wulf Kahan chose, where Kahan Automotriz *is presently located, on 376 Miguel de Cervantes Saavedra, belonged to* Grupo Alfa *and was mortgaged several times:* "Buying it was a huge complication," *remembers notary public José Hernández Patrón,* "it was a real mess, for the land was divided into five lots, and therefore, five different mortgages and five different partnerships were involved as well. My friend Wulf came to me and said:

'I have this problem, what should I do?'
'The best would be for you to get all the land for your whole family.'
What else could a man with such a great heart and tenacity do? He took responsibility of all the debt -a very big debt- and I told him:

'I am sure that with your working technique and that great family of yours, you will do well.' And he certainly did."

It was then that Wulf, Ari, and Jack, the three 'hand in hand', worked hard to buy the property owned by Grupo Alfa *and, although they were in debt up to the eyeballs, they were committed to go on, each in his own way: Jack, who managed to provide the necessary money in cash for this enormous operation, in charge of the Sales Department: Ari, as the company's administrator and motivating the staff: and Wulf presiding over the whole operation, including the company's readjustment and the construction of new facilities on Miguel de Cervantes Saavedra.*

This new dealership is good proof that father and sons can, in deed, be partners for better or for worse, for not much time had passed when, in 1982, Mexico suffers a dramatic change in both economical and political aspects; so, once again, new challenges had to be faced.

The Kahan's decided to try their luck elsewhere and established Kahan Auto-Center, and later on, Sports Arena Dodge, in San Diego, California. Both businesses were Jack's best training along with Wulf's guidance, who started to spend some time in San Diego, and some in Mexico, in order to look after both companies. "It was extremely difficult for me to understand how to do business in another country, but that gave me the chance of learning to face challenges and identify opportunities," *Wulf Kahan used to say.*

Many are the memories of those tough times; and one of those many, is narrated by public accountant, Mr. Saul Delgado: "On February 17, 1982, at the time of the crisis which followed the devaluation of the Mexican peso, Mr. Wulf Kahan called me over and asked how things were at the company: he wanted to know my opinion regarding the situation, so I suggested we sell *Kahan Automotriz*. We were standing in the hallway while we talked, I remember it perfectly, and he immediately answered:

'No, that's impossible; we have overcome other times of crisis, like the one back in 1938, year of the petroleum expropriation, and other very difficult moments, and we are not going to throw more than 55 years of great effort and hard work away just because of five bad years to come. No, we won't sell, we believe in Mexico and we must keep investing in Mexico.'

Some time later, this same posture of his was shown again when the bank industry was taken over by the State in 1982, and he said:

'We still believe in Mexico.'

We can now realize that there is no such thing as easy times, what's important is facing reality and being able to adapt oneself to change, for that is the only constant element in life."

The company at its birth: an employee, Wulf, and Szewel Kahan.

CHAPTER III

The Business

The client is our company's most important visitor.

He is no interruption of our work, he is the purpose of work itself.

He is no stranger in our business, he is a part of it.

We are not doing him a favor (by pleasing him), it is he who is doing us a favor by giving us the opportunity to serve him.

Anonymous

Ever since Szewel Kahan opened his first business, La Europea, *a used car parts shop, which he started with a budget of $200.00 pesos, this philosophy has prevailed in Wulf Kahan's companies:* "A one peso credit is worth more than a pocket-full of cash." *And it is Wulf Kahan himself who now continues explaining the foundations that his business was based on.*

During a speech he gave in 1982, he said: "our main concern is to be the link between the manufacturer and the consumer, with a full understanding of the interests and aspirations of both."

"At Kahan, the client is always our most important visitor and we consider him part of the organization. Thus, all our efforts and the work of our staff are oriented towards that same objective."

"Our financiers are part of the family. Our suppliers are too. It is a big family, you say? Well, of course! And here we are, gathered all to confirm it. But, as we all know, being a numerous family is not enough; what makes our family so special is that we live in harmony with each other, we all have the same objectives, we are devoted to our family, and most of all, we trust one another. I believe that at Kahan trust has been the most important factor for the company's growth."

"The Kahan organization has been dynamic, efficient, and well prepared in all technical aspects. In spite of all this, however, it has been an organization that has placed such things as friendship, ethical principles, commitment, and human relationships above everything else. We have always searched for trust in others and have been a company others can trust."

Ever since 1982, Wulf Kahan has run car and truck dealerships, both in Mexico and the United States. After six years of wonderful experiences, Jack decides to return to Mexico City, rather than because of economical motives, for a family related reason: his father asked him to reconsider the importance of spending some time with his grandparents, uncles and aunts, cousins, and grow and watch his children grow among his family. Thus, Jack joins the "Mexico operation", giving his best to the company, but now, being one more student at the "University of Life".

As Wulf Kahan himself relates in the ideas expressed in the last few paragraphs, he created a true family enterprise. This is confirmed by testimonies such as the one given by Mr. Federico Anaya, who says: "He achieved the most absolute unity among his tribe, the great Kahan family. He set an example for his brothers and children to follow and he loved them dearly. And besides, they all admired his abilities as a leader."

"Considering the workers as part of the family within the company," *continues Dr. Miguel Angel Gil,* "is a characteristic found in union leaders, not in entrepreneurs. If we compare a handful of people descendant from entrepreneurs or politicians, it would be no easy task to find someone with who is socially oriented; as a matter of fact, they would all have a very poor idea of what helping others really is. As a businessman, Wulf Kahan had a true social vocation which he passed on to his children. And that concept of a family oriented organization, not kinship-based but more like a business bond, is very special, in deed."

"There are very successful and important enterprise families, such as Bayer, Coca-Cola, Olivetti, that follow an institutional development policy -a corporate system of involving the workers in the company's objectives. Wulf created a true family enterprise by incorporating people who did not belong to the Kahan family into the company's Administration Council. He wanted to do business and for that he respected each person's individuality. This country would be a whole different story if there were more men like him."

About these same ideas, Jorge Dillman wrote in a newspaper article that "Wulf had inherent leadership abilities, he was a creator of great entrepreneurs. To him, selling vehicles was so much more than a mere commercial transaction; it meant giving a little of himself with every client he took care of; inevitably, there was a trace of him left in every deal he closed."

"Wulf Kahan used to say that the workers' well-being should be one of the businessman's main concerns," *says Mr. Mauricio Rioseco.* "I remember Don Wulf being with the company's employees and mechanics in the repair shop having a drink and toasting with them during the car shows; that's why they liked him. Everyone loved him and he was very respectful of each individual's way of being. I was surprised when I found out that *Kahan Automotriz* closes on December 12[8] and offers a mass for all the staff; that earned him even more the respect of all his employees."

"In 1989, when my father and Don Wulf were still alive, Jack Kahan had the idea of founding a Kahan-Rioseco trust fund in order to donate a university scholarship to a child of one of our staff members. That meant using the company's resources for the good of its own people. Don Wulf was a very daring person and a real fighter with a true commitment to his enterprise."

Mr. Agustín Ochoa has written the following paragraphs:

"Wulf Kahan always knew how to choose his staff and gave them proper training and protection. In the automotive industry, both in Mexico and in the United States, he was a very pleasant person to work with. He always devoted himself to contribute with his knowledge and good disposition to ensure a happy ending to all the surveys Chrysler Detroit needed us to complete: statistics regarding automobile and truck demand in Mexico; about the use of Mopar spare and repair parts; about the establishment and expansion of automotive repair shops; about the used unit sale operation; about the advertising and publicity campaigns; etc."

"He was a very positive element at the reunions the Chrysler dealers held at the plant. We really appreciated his valuable experience. The same situation applies during our visits to Chrysler, Detroit, where everything had a very

---

[8] *The Virgin of Guadalupe Day*

successful outcome. For years, our make was number one on the list, which was a real achievement. If we compare ourselves with the competition, Wulf was really a Chrysler freak, so to speak."

"During the tough times of the automotive industry's integration, Wulf held very important positions and offered his time and effort to see such integration be achieved with intelligence, while the former Chrysler Distributors Association (*Asociación de Distribuidores Chrysler*) collaborated with the *ANDA*, the Automobile Distributors National Association (*Asociación Nacional de Distribuidores de Automóviles*)."

There are quite a few testimonies about Wulf Kahan's performance as a Chrysler dealer, some of which are included in the following paragraphs:

Don Vicente Ariztegui says that "Wulf would deal and do business with Chrysler, Detroit without speaking a word of English. He was a real fighter and a Chrysler man a hundred per cent. He was always one of the important elements in the Association; Guillermo Prieto, Juan Pastrana, and Wulf Kahan were the trilogy."

"I consider Wulf Kahan to be one of the foundation columns of the automotive business, of the Chrysler representation in Mexico. He was one of the first to represent them here."

Mr. Vito Bellifémine tells us that Wulf "was one of the first dealers that came to me since he was one of the first Chrysler distributors."

"We held several conversations during which I would ask him for advice regarding the business atmosphere and he used to be a good counselor. He spoke about business and said we had to do something about the price teasing and it really wasn't easy to find an answer for those things regarding prices."

"I had an automotive, social, and friendship bond with Wulf Kahan," *says Mr. Carlos Doring.* "I can't say it was merely a business relationship; because of the position I held at Chrysler, and him being a distributor for the company, we established a friendship, as well: him, as a Chrysler dealer, and me, as an executive officer in the corporation."

We can appreciate the image of Wulf Kahan as a businessman through all these comments, to which we can add the one made by Mr. Eduardo Orvañanos:

"His dealership was a very active one; you could always find him supervising what was being done at the repair shop, or find him at the plant, or checking the spare parts shop. He gave Mexico his best years."

CPA, Daniel González D'Bejarle continues: "Wulf Kahan's most active moments, where the dealership was concerned, were during the planning of the office building at the new facilities, back in 1981-1982, when they were moving the dealership from Ejército Nacional to its new location. In those times, I was working on a project regarding the conversion of the *Titán* cardboard container factory, which belonged to *Grupo Alfa*, into facilities suitable to the Kahan company's needs. After the Kahan's reached a purchasing agreement, the distribution department, of which I was in charge, had to negotiate the conversion process of the factory into a car dealership agency."

"Wulf Kahan's main concern on this was to make the best use of the available area for the after-sale customer services in the dealership. We used the factory's main building for this; there was a railway platform which was turned into the exhibition room and decided to give the workshop a larger area."

"We needed to relocate *Kahan Automotriz*, then on a leased site on Ejército Nacional. We were asked to vacate the premises and in 1980 we started looking for a place to move the business to. It was thanks to Ari that these great results were achieved; he negotiated with *Alfa*, relocated the dealership very near to where they had been before, and focused on offering the customer the best service possible."

"Wulf was a man preoccupied about satisfying his clients' needs; he was a born entrepreneur who concentrated on maintaining a quality service and making sure the customer received the attention he deserved."

Mr. Agustín Velasco adds that " Mr. Wulf Kahan is a symbol of a whole period in the automotive industry; he was truly identified with Mexico's development concerning that area."

"He left his mark in the automotive field; he was meant to be one of its pioneers. He was a promoter of the automotive sector and helped in the expansion and development of both, the *AMDA*[9] and the industry itself. He was a man who tried to participate in the companies that helped the automotive sector and still does his family, with great love and with no other interest but the industry's well-being. Wulf was an important man during his time; a constructive man who promoted the companies in the sector and created many job sources. He always possessed an entrepreneur's vision and had as many friends as he did family relatives and business deals."

As a businessman, Wulf Kahan was always proud of where he had come from and of having started with barely anything. Mr. Juan José Ortega comments in this respect:

"I will forever remember the *Kahan Automotriz* anniversary celebrations, in which Wulf presented slideshows about his first steps in this important field of activity in the city of Puebla. In these slideshows, he demonstrated the love he had for his family and for the country that had received him hospitably; he was in love with life and his family. Wulf Kahan was very supportive of his children in whatever concerned that new activity, in sickness and in health; during the last years of his life; from that wheelchair of his; but always there to support his children."

"I was very impressed to see the love that the people in his automotive company had for Don Adolfo," *says Dr. Miguel Jusidman*, "especially, those who were the first

[9]   *Spanish initials for the Mexican Association of Automobile Distributors (Asociación Mexicana de Distribuidores de Automotores)*

distributors in the industry would come to him with respect and special affection. I noticed the fondness they had for him. Some even treated him like a patriarch."

Facing the tough moments with optimism and self-confidence was another of Wulf Kahan's characteristics, as Dr. Carlos Rossell Álvarez points out:

"I was a witness to the fact that not everything was success in his business, especially during the ´82-´83 crisis; it was then that I was able to appreciate his great strength in bearing all kinds of problems. He never lost his sense of humor and cheerfulness, although I did see him worry. But there he was, supporting Ari and Jack, and promoting teamwork among his staff; serving as a brace for his family; proving that they had to go on, just as he did. Not giving up, not backing down was crucial for his reaching his goals."

"In 1983, the Chrysler dealers went to the *IPADE*[10] in order to create a counseling plan and help the Chrysler corporation through the difficult times. They needed to analyze real cases that would serve them as examples, based on which they would come up with practical solutions and Wulf authorized that the company's case be presented as an example. Ari had a lot to do with this decision: he trusted the *IPADE* and, in a very active manner, he convinced his father that exposing their case would bring them more good than harm. And besides, the solutions found would benefit all Chrysler dealers."

[10] *Panamerican Institute of Business Executive Managment (Instituto Panamericano de Alta Dirección de Empresas)*

Mr. Manuel Viniegra also comments about Wulf Kahan's performance as a Chrysler dealer: "I met him during the time I was Chrysler's Commercial Director, in the early 80's; although he was going through some rough moments, he was a good businessman. He ran the franchise Chrysler had given him constantly sticking to what the plant said. I remember him to be a very reasonable person to deal with, very solemn when it came to business. He was the typical fighter; very devoted to his company and full of vitality, as well."

Mr. Gilberto Cantú continues: "By 1980, more or less, the Kahan's had to vacate the facilities where their business was located and embarked on a new and huge adventure with Chrysler as they decided to build a dealership of incredible proportions, impelled by us at Chrysler. Maybe, they lost perspective, and a lot of the other distributors were in over their heads."

"When the down fall of the automotive industry trapped us all in 1982-1983, back when they were practically in bankruptcy because the interest rates were sky high and there were no sales, Wulf Kahan would say, 'the situation will get better' and I don't recall ever seeing him alarmed about it. His perseverance was such that things in fact came around and they have turned out well, not only business-wise."

Mr. Oscar Siegal insists on the importance that Wulf Kahan gave his clientele. They had to be completely satisfied with the company's services:

"I used to have a 1957 model automobile and my dad and my father-in-law constantly insisted:

'You should get yourself a new car; you really need a new car.'

'No, first, I have to achieve my economical stability,' I used to say.

'I am a friend of Adolfo's,' said my father-in-law, 'let's go pay him a visit at the dealership on Niño Perdido.'

Once we were at the agency, he said:

'Listen, Adolfo, I'm here to take a look at a car for my son-in-law.'

Then Mr. Kahan turned to me and said:

'So, your father-in-law is going to buy you a car.'

'I wish!,' I answered, 'I am the one who's buying it.'

Although Don Adolfo was a very tough man when it came to business, he affectionately turned to my father-in-law and asked him:

'Let's see, Leoncito (that's how he called him), are you going to buy the car for Oscar or not?'

'No,' he answered.

Then he told him in that joking tone that characterized their friendship, 'Then turn around because I'm going to deal with Oscar. Which one do you like?' he asked me and I showed him the car I liked.

'Look, I'll take your car in exchange for this one and I'll give you six months with no interests to pay for the car.'

'Why?' I asked.

'Because I like you,' he said.

My father loved the car I had chosen and then bought another one just like it. There weren't any speedways back then, there was only the *Viaducto*[11] and right there was where the steering mechanism of my father's car broke. When that happened, he called me and I arrived at the place where the car had broken down, called for a tow truck, and went straight to the dealership. One of the service managers received the car and told me the guarantee was no longer valid. That's when I saw Don Adolfo:

'What's up, Oscar? How are you?'
'The car's steering system broke,' I said, 'thank God my father wasn't hurt, but that manager tells me that the guarantee is not valid anymore.'

He then took the manager by the arm and told him:
'Are you insane? First of all, he's a friend of mine; second, this car was defective; third, thank your lucky stars he's a friend and won't sue us; and fourth, the plant will answer for the car's flaws, and if they don't, we will.'

"I thought, 'the old man is a great guy.' Some time later I got married; then, my son grew up and the moment came to buy him a car. We were thinking of a '75 or '76 two door Valiant and, of course, I visited Adolfo at his new location on Ejército Nacional. Ari was already working there and I said:

---

[11] *One of three important highways in Mexico City.*

'My boy wants a car. Look Ari, I'm very fond of you, but I feel more affection for your dad. Adolfo, I want you to give me the price; this is the car I can afford for my son.'

My son liked the model Adolfo had named *Primavera*, but it was more expensive and I told Adolfo so.

'Buy it for him, then', he said.
'I cannot afford it right now.'
'You just buy it; I'll let you have it for the same price as the other one.'
And so, he gave me the *Primavera* at the same cost as the one I could afford."

"He made me feel really good, especially when I was young; he made me feel as if I were the world's greatest buyer and not like a spoiled kid who once came to see him accompanied by hi father-in-law."

Mr. Jesús Licona affirms that, although Wulf Kahan was a wonderful businessman, money was not the most important thing to him. And so, he tells us about one time he had bought a Valiant "Carnaval" which was given to him with a temporary permit until it got the permanent license plates: "The next Monday, I was driving my children to school when another driver, with no caution whatsoever, pulled out from his garage and hit my car, which had only been driven no more than 21 miles. I immediately went to *Kahan Automotriz* to have it fixed. While I was waiting for someone to take care of me, Mr. Wulf Kahan came up to me and said:

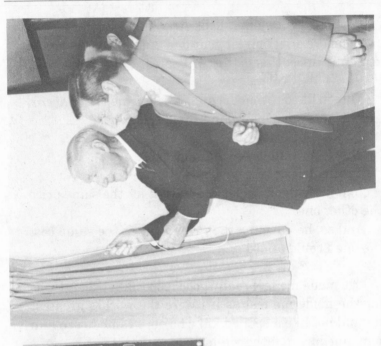

Mr. Gastón Azcárraga Vidaurreta and Wulf Kahan during the inauguration of Kahan Automotriz, S.A. de C.V., in 1969.

'Don't worry, you won't even be able to tell there was a dent there. Thank God that all that with money is bought, with money is repaired.'

Saul Rosales, one of the Service Managers says: "Don Adolfo dreamed of having a car dealership that people would trust; a place where he could welcome his friends and face them in case there were any problems; where they could drop by for a visit and he wouldn't only hear complaints from them."

"He designed a plan and was very much aware that it would take him years and years to carry it out. 'What am I going to do to get the money? What am I going to do? Do the work myself', he thought and continued capitalizing his business and then opened up a more advanced company: *Compañía Impulsora Automotriz de México, S.A. (CIAMSA)* which is still located on the corner of Niño Perdido, No. 33, and Dr. Río de la Loza."

"Then, with the purpose of raising the sales at CIAMSA, the man offered William Sprowls a partnership in the business which did not work out well. The funny thing about it was that it wasn't Mr. Sprowls who Don Adolfo did not get along with, but his children. Everything just got to the point where that partnership could not be any longer, it was against the clients interests and not good in any way for Don Adolfo's health, who almost suffered a heart attack. It was in moments like those that you could really appreciate the kind of man he was; he decided to start a new company of his own and of better quality than the one he was loosing to the Sprowls."

"He asked for a lot of loans and credit. He would start working at seven in the morning and would end up all covered in dust from supervising the construction workers; he would go home just to shower and come right back. He would sit under a beach parasol on the location grounds and sold cars there. If it hadn't been for this, considering the problems that represented paying the loan interest rates, they would've had to stop the construction because they had already invested everything they had and all which they had borrowed."

"Health problems and all, he kept on working...until the day came when the new company's facilities were inaugurated right across the street from the Red Cross hospital and the human resources developed at CIAMSA were now noticeable. I had just joined the company then. The staff fully responded to all his expectations and to the kind of company he wanted to create: one that would answer to his friends trust. I know he wanted to be trustworthy in other people's eyes so as to feel spiritually secure."

"When he left CIAMSA and barely avoided a heart attack, he was so determined to have his own company that he made his decision: 'it's going to have my name, *Kahan Automotriz*, there's my family name and I am going to honor it. There are so many cases in which an enterprise is not doing so well and no one knows who it belongs to; but if I name it Kahan, everyone will know it's mine."

"He carried on with very serious and hard work. In a way, the man really deserves to be honored nationwide."

"I don't want anyone to be harmed in any way, don't you leave anyone without his car", *Don Adolfo would say when vacation time was coming.* "Some of my friends are not taking any more cars in their businesses because vacation time is right around the corner and meanwhile they are hurting a friend's feelings by not taking his car in for service. He had a very special way of speaking:

'I see we have a lot of cars that need repairing, what are we going to do Saul?'

'Don't you worry, sir. I have some mechanics available and we won't leave anyone without a car,' I would say.

'Do you promise we are not leaving anybody without his or her car?'

"We would gather up a group of mechanics and would get to work as much time as it was necessary. One Friday we did not stop until 4 a.m., on Saturday, but we never left a car unrepaired. All were given back to the customer on time. And what did Mr. Kahan do about it? If he had paid us as established by the law, we would have received what corresponded to the extra hours we had spent working; instead, he actually gave us 30 per cent more, which was in fact three times what the law indicates."

"Don Adolfo loved going to Acapulco on a V-8 Dodge with two four-throat carburetors, but since that car wouldn't reach Acapulco on just one full tank, he would have to stop for gas in Tierra Colorada and fill the tank up again. The time I gave the car a tune up, he said after he had come back from his trip:

'Let's 'see, who tuned up my car? Have him come to my office.'

'Who knows what is wrong with the car,' Mr. Ronquillo said to me. So I went to the office and Don Adolfo asked me:

'Are you new here?'

'Yes, sir. I was the person who gave the car a tune up.'

'And where did you learn to do it?'

'Me?, well, at school,' I answered.

Then he said, 'Look, my car would only go to Tierra Colorada with a full tank. I thought there was something wrong with the pump at the gas station because the car only took very little gas and now it is running like clockwork. I stopped for gas on the way back and filled it up with practically nothing; I still have half a tank full. It's not consuming that much gasoline now and I couldn't make it with one full tank before.' And he congratulated me on my work."

"Another time, there was a big problem with the Chrysler General Manager's car: something was wrong with it and Don Wulf took the risk of telling him to send it to us so we could repair it. And we did. Mr. Victor Montalvo couldn't believe it; he took the car out for a test drive one Saturday and on Sunday we received a recognition for our work."

"We, the workers, were a little grain of sand that contributed to make Don Adolfo's dream come true: an exemplary company that would make it possible for him to welcome his friends anytime. There was no secretary to keep you from walking into his office. He made his dream come true and worked for more than 60 years."

"At *Kahan Automotriz* we worked to solve many problems. During all those years, I only recall one time when we didn't share the same opinion about something, in the technical area, that is, not in anything that had to do with management or the staff. After checking a car Don Adolfo told me:

'Saul, that you are saying is wrong; I've never heard such an outrageous thing in my life. I don't think you are right this time.'

There was a problem with a car belonging to *Banamex*'s Purchasing Manager but he could not put his finger on what it was exactly. I asked him something and then, before the client, I told Mr. Adolfo:

'It's the rims,' and he said:
'What Saul is saying makes no sense at all. Please, let's step in my office…Let us keep your car for one week in order to repair it.'

"That time Don Adolfo did not send for me, but it was him who personally went looking for me at the workshop, and I told him what was wrong with the vehicle."

'I still think that what you are saying is nonsense, but if you think so, go ahead.'

"I had the rims leveled and put them back on the car. Mr. Adolfo, along with his brother Luis and Mr. Victor, took the car out for a test drive that Saturday. They drove almost to Querétaro, turned around and on the way back, the man said:

'It looks like it's all right now,' and it was."

Mr. Fernando Cohen, who participated more recently with Wulf Kahan, says: "I met Mr. Kahan many years ago, around 1963, but we stopped seeing each other for a long time. Around 1990, my father, Samy Cohen, my brothers, Luis, Raymundo and Carlos, and I, suggested that we form a partnership with the Kahan's who said they already had an established business but wanted to share it with us."

"Mr. Kahan had already established this Nissan dealership, here in Interlomas; he always arrived at seven in the morning and wouldn't leave until eight or nine at night; he would step out to grab some lunch and came right back. He was a very dynamic individual, with a very special personal charm but very strict as well. His way of working was very impressive."

In the comment made by Mr. Jorge Maldonado he also talks about the Kahan Nissan dealership in Interlomas: "Through out those months, I was constantly in touch with Don Wulf and realized that his idea of running the construction was based on a practical point of view -the creation of systems and comfortable areas for his clients within the building; I saw it from a more theoretical angle and enjoyed every tour I made with Don Wulf around the grounds and the construction site. I learned that being analytical and profound before expressing an opinion is of great importance. I, that spoke based on theoretical concepts, was surprised at the profoundness of his thoughts and realized how valuable his ideas were. The final conclusion of all this is that one's thoughts need to be deeper and more analytical before saying anything. What is certainly true is that he was very thoughtful when it came to the clients."

After sixteen years of intense labor, from 1977 to 1992, only death could dissolve the partnership Wulf Kahan had formed with his children. Financial businesses, leasing companies, and more automobile dealerships, of all makes, at larger scale, and all over the country, were born even during Wulf's illness years; at the end, they also got involved in the Mexican banking system. All this emerged from one single phrase inherited from Szewel Kahan: "A one peso credit is worth more than a pocket-full of cash."

Thank God, Wulf Kahan lived to see companies and job sources be born and grow, and which we hope will still be motive of 'naches'[12] *for him, wherever he may be.*

---

[12] *Hebrew word for rejoice, happiness, enjoyment.*

Saul Rosales presenting Wulf Kahan with an acknowledgment
on behalf of the company's workers.

CHAPTER IV

The Boss

Pay the worker for the job he has done
before he wipes the sweat from his forehead.

Anonymous.

Now I realize how little I truly knew my father as a boss. I was aware that his employees appreciated him, but I did not know many things about him that were brought to light through the interviews held for the making of this book. Some of the people that, for one reason or another, worked for Wulf Kahan contributed with a few lines which, in this chapter, describe him as a boss.

"I met him lots of years ago. I started working at the Deportivo Israelita[13] in 1954; I used to wash cars back then and my relationship with Don Adolfo started at the same time when I was learning to drive. It seemed to me that he was a very simple person," *says Javier Castellanos,* "quiet, and straight forward in his way of treating other people, in the way he spoke. That I can recall, he was never ever disrespectful towards me, never humiliated me, or treated my badly. Never. He had a car dealership then called *Impulsora Automotriz*, located on the corner of Niño Perdido and Fray Servando; and me... at barely eighteen years old, I was already thinking about getting myself a car:

'Mr. Adolfo, do you have used cars in your business?'
'Yes, we also sell used cars at the dealership; if you wish, you can go take a look sometime, just don't mention my name. Just drop by and let someone show you the cars and tell you their price.'

A salesman took care of me there; he showed me a car and I told him I wanted 'a little credit'.
'Do you have a house of your own? A guarantor?' he asked.

[13] *The Jewish community sports center*

My hopes of getting a car crumbled to the ground, and then I told the man I would try to find myself a guarantor. Back at the sports club Don Adolfo asked me:

'So, did you go already?'

'Yes sir.'

'And what happened?'

'The truth is I think I'm not ever going to have a car,' I said.

'Why is that?' he asked.

'They asked me for a guarantor, something that would answer for me in case I couldn't pay.'

'Did you see the car you would like to have?'

'Yes, sir.'

'Come by again on Monday.'

So I went there on Monday and all of a sudden, I saw Don Adolfo with his famous pipe, which had a deliciously aromatic vanilla-scented tobacco, and said in that accent of his:

'Hi! How are you?'

'Fine, sir.'

'Hold on, I'll be right with you. How much money do you have for the car?'

Back then, there was a little car called Simca. Its cost was $18,000 pesos, and I told him:

'I have $4,500 pesos.'

'O.K., I'll see what I can do for you. You ask your mom or dad to sign the papers as your guarantor. You'll sign the credit letters for $400 or $500 pesos each; will you be able to pay this way?'

"Yes, sir,' I answered.

I earned ten pesos a day plus tips in those times, and when I came here, to the Golf Club, I was already making twenty pesos a day, plus tips. The truth is I never forgot that favor he did for me. I kept seeing him once in a while after I relocated here at the Golf Club."

Anita Hernández, one of Wulf Kahan's secretaries, who worked for him during nine years, says:

"As a boss, Don Adolfo was a very strict person. I learned so much from him; thanks to him, I matured and learned the ways of a secretary. And as a human being and a friend, he was really incredible. In my heart, he is still alive."

"The advice Don Adolfo gave me was like a father's advice to his daughter; he guided me whenever I had a decision to make, in helping me become a responsible person. I remember one day I was just standing here in the hallway; it had just stopped raining and I was looking at the hills in the background; I was miles away, and he asked me:

'What are you staring at, Anita?'
'I'm nurturing my spirit,' I answered.
'Wouldn't you love to be able to see what's behind those mountains?' he asked again.
'Yes, sir,' I said.
'That means you are a restless person, that you are capable of doing many things and that is a quality which is only acquired through time. You have the ability to climb

to the highest mountain top, you can fulfill your dreams; don't be afraid.'

"Whenever he started telling me about his former jobs, he proved to me that anyone can find any type of work hard to do, but making the road either a difficult one or an easy one, depends only on each one of us."

"One of the things I admired most about him was his attitude towards life. He was such a capable man that he never gave up on anything; he had the ability of doing a lot of different things. Besides, he was a man of strong character. His personality commanded attention and respect and it showed even in his walk."

"One day, on Mr. Ari's birthday, we decided to throw him a party. We thought Mr. Wulf would be bothered by it because we even brought a mariachi band to the celebration. When the band had arrived and they wouldn't start playing, he stared at us and said:

'Why isn't the band playing? Is something wrong?'
'Mr. Wulf,' I said, 'we are here to celebrate Mr. Ari's birthday,' and I tried to explain myself to him but he was not upset, on the contrary."

"And during the party, Mr. Ari sang *Viejo, mi querido viejo*[14] in such an emotional manner, we were all deeply moved by it."

[14] *Song which the author wrote in honor and dedication to his father, a man of old age; the title meaning: My old man, my dear old man.*

'I've had many pleasant evenings,' Mr. Wulf commented, 'but now, this moment will forever stay in my mind and soul because my son dedicated and sang this song to me.'

"He was a most intelligent and extremely wise man; so astute in business that he knew exactly which deals would work out fine. Regarding internal matters, with just taking a look at whatever was wrong, he'd immediately pin point the problem. He taught us to take good care of the clients and made us realize that this job source, *Kahan Automotriz*, existed thanks to our customers. He tried his best to build solid foundations for his company so, when he was no longer with us, the business could go on. He used to tell me:

'Even if the earth shakes everything down to its core, Anita, even if the earth shakes, this is so solidly built that nothing will ever happen to it. Always remember that each client that leaves here dissatisfied is not ever coming back, and everything we have, we owe to every one of them. Success is based on always doing things the correct way. Whatever you do, if it is done right, it will never fall apart.'

"He would get angry about things, but wouldn't scold people over just anything. He would say 'that happened because of this and the result is now so and so,' or also 'why are you doing things backwards? Think well before you start doing it.' That's why no one contradicted him. He used to be right most of the time. He liked us to be orderly and would sometimes stop right in the middle of an assignment:

'No, no, let's see... all of you, line up.' And then he would put all our things in a line as well and say 'this is your file cabinet, this is where all your documents and files should be; make it look like an office should look like. Things should always be done correctly, and the better they are done, the faster you'll reach your goal.'

"I was very impressed by Mr. Adolfo's personality. The truth is that at first I was scared of him, but once I started having more contact with him, I realized he was an incredible human being."

"When ever he came back from a trip, he would always bring me a little present and it felt nice to know I was an important part of his life, that I was not just another secretary, but a collaborator in the enterprise. He really motivated me, so much that I would say to myself 'I'm not only a secretary, I'm truly important to him'."

"I felt terrible when he became ill; I cried a lot and prayed to God to give him that special strength he needed to go on. It was just not fair that such an intelligent man, a nice man, who was always concerned about his people, had become so sick."

'And my people?' he'd say, 'What's going to happen with my people?' He would also tell me: 'I know that someday I'm not longer going to be here, but always remember Anita, when there is an obstacle blocking the road, you should always fight hard to overcome it and never give up.'

"That man's nature, so strict, so solemn, so stable, changed when he fell ill. He let people hug him, he wanted to be pampered, to be spoiled. He was like the granddaddy I never had. He was so full of so many nice things..."

"There was this one time when we took out his pictures of a long time ago and he was telling me the names of all his friends, and I asked him:

'When do we start writing your memoirs?'
'I don't want us to do it,' he would say, 'let others take care of that; I only left something here for other people to write about it.'

"He wanted history to be the only judge about whether he had been right or wrong throughout his life. From time to time I would ask him when would we start writing, and he'd answer:

'No, I'm not writing anything; others will surely take care of that.

"Don Adolfo was a great motivation for me. Thanks to him, I was able to buy my first car, which cost me then $3'000,000 pesos. I had already set my eyes on it, but I only had $1'000,000 pesos and told him I could only spend that amount for the time being."

'I'll think about it.'
"I had thought that he would surely forget about it, but the next day he told me:

'I already took care of it.'

So they gave me the car. While I drove it, I felt as if I was in another world."

"One day, I got the opportunity of buying another piece of land aside from the one I already owned. I needed more money to buy this other property, so I sold my car and bought the land. I thought Mr. Kahan would be upset about it, but to my surprise, he told me that that way I would have something to support myself with."

Some family members of his who also worked for the company, give their opinion as well about Wulf Kahan as a boss:

Samuel Kahan comments: "When the dealership was located on Ejército Nacional, I held the position of Administrative Manager and we had a very tight relationship, for he was not only my uncle, but my boss as well. If I wanted to take some time off for vacations, I had to ask Don Adolfo for permission. I think that extraordinary talent he had for doing business, he inherited from my grandfather."

"There were times when we did have heated discussions, however, after arguing our relationship remained unharmed; on the contrary, it grew stronger. We had a very emotional bond between us: we cried together and we hugged each other."

"He was a good man. When one of his employees wanted to talk to him, it was not necessary for the person to set an appointment or wait for long, in fact, I hardly recall the door to his office ever being closed. He liked to keep it open all the time."

"He would scold us for arriving late to work since he was always the first there. He was very disciplined, nevertheless, he was open to others' opinions and was willing to change things when convenient. Things weren't only done his way just because he had said so; he would take opinions from other people, even though the Kahan's are famous for being quite stubborn."

Arie Derzavich tells us what he thinks about his grandfather as a boss:

"When I was about 15 years old, I worked here in his business at the spare parts department for a period of two months, more or less. I noticed that everyone had a lot of respect for him. I remember him being very busy all the time; he always had something to do, a goal to reach, and this was an everyday situation. His goals were not only long term ones."

"There were a lot of times that I accompanied him to the golf course and I realized he had a very good time playing the sport. He had a marvelous sense of humor, he knew how to enjoy every single moment of it; it was as if nothing else existed, just the things that made each moment special. He lived life to the last degree, every instant, he did what he wanted and that permitted him and his family to enjoy life together."

"During one's life, there are examples that you wish to follow; he has been my role model, my example. Thanks to all I realized about him while I was an employee here, I can now behave appropriately at my present job, everything from knowing how to talk to people to have them follow instructions and respect me at the same time, to knowing how to be a good human being. That is what I most admire about my grandfather's personality. Being here helped me realize exactly where I come from and what I should expect from life, how to set goals for myself, how to talk to an employee, even how to lay him off, not hurting his feelings, but in a friendly manner. All that is now very helpful to me."

Also Perla, Wulf Kahan's daughter, worked at the dealership, at the cashier's window; she held the job for approximately one year and says: "He treated me like just any another employee; My working schedule started at nine in the morning and he was very strict about us arriving to work on time."

"He never used his friends to get something; he'd always work long and hard to obtain what he wanted. He was very constant in saving his money: if he earned one peso, he would save 50 cents and would manage to do with the other 50. Later, when the economic situation improved, he would make donations to different charity institutions, for social causes, or anything which meant helping his fellow man, helping the needy."

Mr. Francisco Miranda mentions as well that "Wulf always kept in mind that work makes a man's life more valuable, and that it is man himself who makes work an honorable thing. Remembering this, one may achieve true self-fulfillment in life and Wulf sure practiced these concepts."

Saul Rosales, the union's leader, tells us about Wulf Kahan:

"As an entrepreneur, as a boss, and as a man of human relations, he did an exemplary job which people should consider following. The man sometimes found himself facing big conflicts with the CIAMSA workers' union; nevertheless, when we had a problem, when we had a death in a worker's family, he would personally go to that employee's home, which was maybe made of just cardboard boxes, and give the family his condolences. He would come to the workers in the union and would ask them to collect 'all the money you can and I will pitch in the same amount; let's see how willing you all are to help your fellow worker.' And that great human quality of his is worth millions."

"He was a man with great concern for his people; he used to say that his employees should earn a living without having to go through economical jams. Mr. Adolfo wanted two thirds of the company's income to be used for salaries and expenses, and the one third which was left would be the enterprise's profit. This was a good motivation because it represented a golden rule that most companies hardly ever follow."

"The employees at Kahan could form a long line with their own cars -and I am also talking about the electricians, mechanics, etc.- which talks very highly about Don Adolfo, about how he respected other people not only verbally speaking. He always helped his workers, but he never gave anything away. True, he did make things easier for us. He never gave things out for free, not to anyone, but he gave each person what he thought he or she deserved for the effort put into their work."

"There was once a problem with some restless boys in the union and I was ordered to intervene because a union representative was coming over and it was possible that the situation could have gotten out of hand. Things were red-hot. Don Adolfo asked me to go on his behalf and:

'Without hurting anyone's feelings, go and solve that problem. Whatever you say, goes.'

"I went to the union representative and he accompanied me. He knew the workers were all on Don Adolfo's side and many appreciated him very much, and that only two or three of them had gotten out of line. When we arrived, there was yelling, and swearing, and insulting all over the place. We sat down and I said:

'I come here on behalf of Mr. Adolfo Kahan; I will give you whatever you are asking for, and will do it exactly the way you ask me to.'

Suddenly, everyone started to quiet down and the silence grew. The union representative's face turned white as he was pulling on me, making sure no one noticed, but I calmed him down:

'You just stay calm. Don't you know already how people are?' And I turned to the boys and said:

The company's employees receiving tableware sets, a gift from Wulf and Ari Kahan.

'Ask for anything. All you have to do is ask.'
'That is just too good to be true,' they answered.
'It is, Mr. Adolfo gave me his word.'

"They did not want to believe me, but I assured them that it was true. Then they asked the union representative and me to step out while they took some time to talk it over."

"They spent more than one hour discussing the matter and the gentleman with me said:

'How could you think of doing such a thing? What are we going to tell Don Adolfo?'

'Don't you worry about it,' I said and a few moments later the workers called us in.
'Come in, we have an answer.'
'Tell me, what is it that you request?' I asked.
'We don't want anything.'
'O.K. then,' said the union representative 'if you don't want anything, there is nothing further to say.'
'Why aren't you asking for anything?' I interfered.
'Because if we do, he's going to give us what we ask for, but he is also going to demand that we work more and, the truth, we are well paid as it is. If we can get a bonus in reward for our efforts, that'll be fine.'

'How much do you want then?' I insisted.
'What ever you determine will be O.K.'
"This shows, in a very realistic way, what Don Adolfo meant to his people. Unfortunately, there are not many

people like him in this world; he was an exceptional man, in every sense of the word."

"I doubt there is another businessman who would do something like this. Don Luis Kahan and Mr. Ari were both very surprised, but Don Adolfo just smiled because he knew the workers were on his side and it was only those two or three who were being rebellious. Firing them would have been the easy way out, but he did not want to harm anyone and that is why the way we solved the problem came as no surprise to him."

"Staying attentive to what was going on back stage was Don Adolfo's main objective; being able to face his friends, not making more money as just any other entrepreneur does. The man was an excellent human being. The love of his people says a lot about what kind of boss he was. He was always gentle, not forceful in any way when treating his employees."

"Don Adolfo used to give me a present every year. Back then, the law did not require the employers to give their workers a Christmas bonus, but every year, he gave me an envelope which I would give to my wife and tell her: 'Here, Don Adolfo sends you this.' That's why I say the man left us a whole different country from the one he knew. The people who were wise enough to appreciate him used to say that he knew what he was doing, that he was not the kind of person who gives up on things. He would gladly give his card to anyone who left the company to look for another job which was a very good reference to have."

"If an employee in the workshop felt afraid when he saw Don Adolfo arrive, it was only because he knew he had not done a good job on repairing a car and if there was one thing Don Adolfo demanded from his people was for them to do quality work."

"The only time we disagreed on anything concerning technical matters was the first time that the man gave out a written guarantee which stated that if a car was not perfectly repaired, he would give the client a new one."

'Saul, can I sign this guarantee letter?' he said.
'Yes, sir.'

"The people that worked for Mr. Adolfo trusted him very much. He would tell us:

'If you mess up, here I am right behind you, to back you up in any way, to help you.' That was why his staff responded in the best way possible.

"Don Adolfo did not accept any flattering from anyone: 'You tell me anything, as long as it is comes straight from the shoulder. I don't want to hear anyone kissing up to me.'

"If he caught anybody in a crooked move, it was enough if that person repented for his actions in order for Don Adolfo to forgive him: 'Let's give him another chance,' he'd say."

"The fact of intentionally harming someone never crossed Don Adolfo's mind. Once, there was a problem with this mechanic who was in charge of a truck ramp area and would sometimes come back to work after having one too many drinks during lunch time. One day, Don Adolfo was passing by while he was driving a truck onto the ramp. The truck was staggering and it began to tilt dangerously. I even thought it was going to turn over anytime."

"Why didn't you use the support beams?' asked Don Adolfo as he pushed the truck to keep it from falling over. It was about to collapse and he said: 'Help him bring it down, hurry!'"

"I was scared and ran because I felt the truck was going to fall right on top of him. Mr. Kahan wasn't afraid of anything. Now that's what I call appreciating and enjoying life as it should be; that is a very valuable attitude in life."

Mr. Arturo Gutiérrez comments that Wulf Kahan was "a promoter of labor awareness, who did not limit himself to paying his employees the best salaries, but also tried to give opportunities to those who really deserved them. This way of running his business placed him fifteen years ahead of his time, since he was already handling the concepts of productivity and efficiency."

"On one occasion, during a Christmas toast ceremony, he went up to his staff and said:

'Right now there's no boss, we are all friends here.'

"It was a very moving moment in which we realized that there was, in fact, a respectful and affectionate relationship between the boss and his staff."

One of Wulf's workers, Mr. Fernando Castro, says that "Mr. Adolfo would come to the workshop and would ask for someone in particular to work on his car and I would always be in charge of repairing and checking all the car's electric system."

"He knew his business quite well and one could never fool him:

'What are you doing?'
'This, Mr. Adolfo.'
'No, you are doing it all wrong; it has to be done this other way,' and he would show the person how it was done."

"One had to speak correctly and with the truth. He was really nice; in any other jobs people are afraid of their boss, but I did not feel afraid of Mr. Adolfo, nor did I ever run and hide if I saw him coming."

"One day he caught me taking a coffee break at around ten in the morning, and while I was eating a roll of bread I tried to ask him:

'May I help you, sir.?'

And then I felt I had to cough since I had stuck the whole role in my mouth and I thought: 'Boy, am I in trouble now.' Then I coughed and even Mr. Adolfo patted me on the back. When I had finished my coffee, I went up to his office and said:

'I'm sorry about that, sir. I was eating because I left my house this morning without having breakfast.'

'Don't worry, there is no problem; you can take a coffee break.'

"In other companies you would surely get in trouble for little things; he was not like that. Sometimes, he even kind of joked around with us:

'But you are always so clumsy...don't tell me you actually know how to fix that.'

"And I would stop and think if he had really meant it or not. There were times when he called for me and I was working on a car, so I had to clean my hands and it would take me a bit long to get to him. Then he would say something like 'if you take so long the next time I call you here, I'm going to send the police to come and get you, you just wait and see.'

There is also some evidence about his way of treating the employees and staff at the AMDA:

"Don Wulf asked me on my first day of work at AMDA: 'And who are you?' he said politely, 'What's your name?'

"That man's personality shocked me, and with a nervous stutter I answered: 'My name is Norberto Cortés, at your service.' He stood up, shook my hand, and said:

'I'm Wulf Kahan and I'm your friend.'

"His treatment towards me touched me deeply because he actually stood up and shook my hand. I remember him as if he was right in front of me now: a strong man, with an impressive look on those green or rather grayish eyes of his."

"I was really moved by the man. It was the first time he'd seen me in his entire life and I don't know what he saw in me that made him act that way. I felt something special inside and said to myself: 'this is going to be an awesome job if everyone here is like this.' I don't mean to make fun of him but he did have a special way of speaking and he would tell me:

'How ar*gh* you Nogbegto? How is it going?'
'Very well, Don Wulf,' I would say as he signed the reports I gave him.

"I was promoted several times since my first job as an office boy and when he took the position as AMDA's Treasurer, his first noble and beautiful deed towards me was giving me a salary raise:

'Nogbegto, you are going to make a bit more money because you deserve it. There's nothing to thank me for, keep working and you will have more,' he told me when I got my raise."

"I always received a first class treatment from Don Wulf. He helped me economically by giving me those raises. He established an incentive for the staff -the after-convention gratification; he would reward both, the people who attended the conventions, and those who for some reason stayed home but had worked as well before the event. Each person would receive a certain percentage based on their salary and that was a good means of motivation."

"Don Wulf had a thorough control over everything and in the Council meetings he would render a detailed report and knew by heart how much money would be gathered through the convention. He was very demanding, but I think that what a boss demands from his staff is in the staff's best interests, as well."

"And he always welcome me with a hug, wherever we met he would greet me with a hug. Sometimes he would address me in a very polite manner and sometimes he would talk to me as if we were long time friends. Nevertheless, he always treated me very nicely and I only remember good things about Don Wulf; even if it doesn't sound respectful enough, that's how I called him, Don Wulf."

"He was already ill when he received me in his office and hugged me with his one good arm and said:

'How are you boy?' Check it out, I'm 62 years old and he called me *boy*."

Laurita González, AMDA's secretary tells us:

"I remember we were at one of the Association's conventions and we had to collect the entrance tickets at the closing ceremony dinner; the staff had a special table assigned and when we were finally able to take our seats, the first course had already been served. The waiter told us that he could not serve us the soup so he would just bring us the main course dish. Mr. Wulf was passing by as this happened and he told the waiter:

'You give these people a red carpet treatment for they are very important to me. Do me the favor of heating the soup up and serving it to them.'

"We told him right away:

'No, sir, please don't worry about it,' but he said again: 'You are very important people to me, let them take good care of you.' And he never stopped worrying about his staff being treated right."

One of AMDA's lawyers, Mr. Federico Anaya, affirms that Wulf Kahan "had a great sense of justice which he showed the few times we had problems at the AMDA. There were two or three unpleasant situations with some disloyal people but Wulf always insisted that he did not want to hurt anyone's dignity. Even when he knew they were nothing but thieves, he did not want them to be harmed in any way."

At home, with the servants, he was also very careful not to hurt their feelings and would always treat them with respect. A friend of the family, Dr. Carlos Rossell says that "the way he treated his servants...I saw him give orders, but never hurt anyone. All those people that worked for him were very fond of their boss and proof of it is the long time they stayed with him...he never hurt or offended them."

Fernando Rosas, who has been the Kahan family's chauffeur for more than 25 years, comments that he felt "like part of the family, as if Mr. Adolfo and Mrs. Estela were my parents, and I say this openly because those are my true feelings, I'm not lying. Don Adolfo loved to eat out; he especially liked *flautas*[15] and *maciza*[16] and sausage tacos. There he'd be, smelling of Halston cologne and wearing his shirts unbuttoned to let his chest show, and would always want me to eat first."

'Come, let's go grab some tacos; go on, eat, eat well boy.'

Professor Guillo Maldonado, his therapist, who only knew him as a sick man, says:

"Wulf Kahan helped me become strong to fight against adversity, to not let myself drown in my own ego during the important moments of life."

"When humble people, like myself, meet a person from the opulent class, we feel less, but when I met Wulf, I found someone I could actually talk to. For others, I'm only the

---

[15] *Deep fried tacos usually made of cheese, chicken, mashed potatoes, refried beans, or barbecued beef.*
[16] *Lean pork meat.*

professor, but not for him. He would introduce me to everyone, he liked to get along with people, not being individualized. I consider it a real privilege to know someone like him."

"Other people like that, from the upper class, are blind regarding the people in the lower classes; it's not that they mean to be rude, but they live in a crystal box and he was just not like that. He would often invite me for breakfast at his home or take me along when he had lunch with other important people."

"For Wulf, every person was important; he listened to what everyone had to say, for example, the boy who fixed the weight training machines at the gym. He never considered others to be less than him and that is what drove everybody to him. While I waited at the gym where he had his therapy every day, other people would ask me about that man who was so nice and so courteous with everyone, and it wasn't until later that they would find out who he was. That is how he won the affection of all the people who knew him."

Wulf and Estela Kahan at an
AMDA Convention (1956).

CHAPTER V

AMDA

Asociación Mexicana
de Distribuidores de Automotores[17]

---

[17] *See footnote 9*

Enthusiasm is what moves the world.

Without its driving force, nothing that is worth doing has ever been achieved.

It eases the sorrows of poverty and the boredom of opulence. Without it, joy cannot be.

Therefore, it must be handled with diligence and used in good judgment.

It is madness to disdain it; true disaster if misused.

Anonymous.

Someone said that AMDA was Wulf Kahan's fiancée because of the love and time he always dedicated to it.

He first came in contact with the Asociación Mexicana de Distribuidores de Automotores (AMDA) *in 1945 and the relationship he then started with the Association would only end with Wulf Kahan's death. He held various positions at the AMDA: from 1970 to 1971 he functioned as Treasurer, and in 1972, he was named First vice-President. He also held the post of President of the Convention Committee in repeated occasions.*

"We were very good friends; almost 40 years have gone by since I first met him," *says Mr. Francisco Plancarte.* "Back then, the AMDA was called *ANDA, Asociación Nacional de Distribuidores de Automóviles*[18]. Nevertheless, our ANDA existed long before the artists' *ANDA*[19], but still, a lot of people used to mistake us for the other institution and I remember commenting on that with other fellow members of the Association. Some other person told Wulf it would be convenient to change the Association's name to AMDA as to avoid someone mistaking him for Doña Sara García[20]. And so, we retired from the possible polemic this would cause and left the field open for our country's actors. After this, we became the AMDA."

[18] *National Association of Automobile Distributors*
[19] *Actors National Association (Asociacion Nacional de Actores)*
[20] *Famous Mexican actress who was known as "Mexico's grandmom".*

"I remember one of the first conventions in the city of Guadalajara, it must have been in '56 or '57 (I had joined the AMDA in 1953); it was a very lively convention and among the many social events, we had a *Palenque*.[21] We were all quite excited that Wulf and Estelita had shown up at the event, him dressed in a *charro* suit and her in a *china poblana* outfit.[22] Although he had not been born in Mexico, he was the only one there who had the great idea of buying a *charro* outfit and actually wearing it to the convention."

"During many years, Wulf was a member of the Board of Directors acting as AMDA's treasurer. He became the substitute for his great friend Don Lorenzo Sours, who served as treasurer for a long period of time. Wulf looked after the Association's interests and moneys with the same diligence as Don Lorenzo did. They were both so strict regarding the expenses that they would constantly tighten the stipend."

"I have been the Association's legal advisor (besides from working for the plant as well) since 1953. With my consent, Mr. Federico Anaya S. was invited to work as one of AMDA's lawyers to especially take care of labor issues and there was one time that the Association invited my son Francisco, being specialized in Corporate Law and Defense, to act as our lawyer before the Consumer Protection Department. As I say once again, Wulf always looked after AMDA's money at all costs."

[21] *Mexican traditional cock fight and show.*
[22] *Both the charro and the china poblana suits are the typical mexican outfits equivalent to a cowboy's festive attire.*

Mr. Jorge Garibay Romanillos remembers having met Wulf Kahan in 1964, when the Association's offices were located on the corner of Reforma Ave. and the street of Morelos; "He was well known in AMDA for his friendly and willing spirit in all he did," *he affirms.*

"In all my years as a distributor, -more than 27- and as a member of the AMDA," *adds Mr. Carlos Krestchmer,* "I always considered Mr. Wulf to be a man who was in love with the Association and noticed that he devoted a lot of time, work and affection to it. I have met very few men in the same field of work who have given so much of themselves to this association. It is pretty much thanks to him that we have the modern facilities at Mercaderes St., where AMDA is located nowadays; he had been appointed as the man in charge of remodeling the place. Actually, the boardroom still looks like it was back when he had just remodeled it; you can say he practically did it with his own two hands...he would spend whole hours supervising the work, and that's an understatement."

"I had the opportunity of traveling abroad several times with my friend Wulf on the occasion of the AMDA conventions; we also attended a few seminars and did some research studies together. I especially remember our trip to New Orleans. My wife was traveling with me that time and it was then when I met Estela; the four of us spent very special moments together during the few days of our trip. We attended as well the National Dealers Association Convention in the U.S. for which we were named Mexico's representatives. After this, I made some other trips with him to Washington, D.C., and Montreal; these are the ones

I remember best. All throughout these trips, he showed me his abilities in union politics and proved to be a true promoter of friendship."

"In 1969, some time after my father passed away, Wulf Kahan phoned me," *remembers Mr. Federico Anaya,* "and asked me to meet him at the dealership. The thought that he was most probably going to tell me he no longer required my services did cross mind since it had already happened with other clients who canceled the contract when they knew my father was gone. But, much to my surprise, Wulf told me:

'Mr. Carlos Bandala, AMDA's General Director, wants you to work as one of the Association's lawyers.' He offered me a salary of $2,000 pesos a month and from that moment on, we started what is now a very tight friendship."

"I will never be able to thank him enough for the opportunity he gave me. He was like a tutor and a father to me; I liked watching the way he acted and learned to appreciate many things about him: his personal charm, his extraordinary human quality...It would be very hard thinking of AMDA's existence without him having been a part of it."

"He was a promoter and a leader. He could have been President of the Association; he probably never was because he did not master the Spanish language, but he did try to promote his candidacy once. Everything he ever did for AMDA, he did willing to serve the Association and came straight from his heart."

"He really liked organizing the AMDA conventions because, besides everything else, Wulf had an amazing love for the city port of Acapulco, for sailboats, and adored the sea. Most of the conventions, which were incredibly well organized, took place in that seaport."

"He felt he had an obligation towards all the people who worked with him and when things were going well, it was great for everyone. There are other bosses who want win other people's respect by force and there's the ones who win it because they are appreciated by their staff; this was Wulf's case. He was always working hard for AMDA," *adds Mr. Norberto Cortés,* "always looking after the Association's interests."

There are a lot of comments about him having been a part of the Association, like the one made by Mr. Emilio Sánchez Peláez, who says: "Wulf was very enthusiastic when it came to the organization. During my presidency at the AMDA, I think he was serving as treasurer then, he suggested that along with the conventions, we should have a showing of the product we sell: cars, trucks, and everything concerned with automobile dealerships."

"At first, when he said he wanted to be in charge of that new project, he encountered a very hostile situation with the rest of the members. But now, that project is one of our main events during the year; for example, we are going to have a showing at the *Hipódromo de las Américas* race track, on November 12, 1992, and let's face it, Wulf deserves the credit for being the one who started these exhibitions, as well as for organizing our conventions in different parts of the country."

"All the employees at AMDA liked him very much; the manager, the secretaries, everyone. He was a very kind man, a very decent man; very strict, he didn't accept things that were done incorrectly, but he was a boss who treated everyone right and had his feet firmly on the ground."

"Being AMDA board members, we once traveled to some place in the U.S., I think it was Las Vegas, where the NADA, National Dealers Association, (AMDA's sister association with 22,000 members) was holding a reunion. They are very solemn people, pretty square, too, and Wulf told them:

'On behalf of the Mexican Association, I would like to send you all our best regards.'

"And he stood before the 16,000 people who attended the event, with a microphone in his hand, without speaking a word of English, and having the support of the only one other Mexican colleague there. And he made it through the acid test because he had set his mind on it; he managed to communicate with them."

Mr. Juan Ortega continues saying:

"During the time I held the position of General Director at AMDA, I always received Wulf Kahan's support through his experience and love for AMDA and all Chrysler associations."

"I remember the conversations we used to have in his office and those photos of his...He would tell me about

From left to right: Luis Kahan, Franz Hammecker, Wulf Kahan, Guillermo Egea Mier, Juan Pastrana, Guillermo Prieto Pérez, Gregorio Pírez, Gastón Azcárraga Tamayo, Vicente Aríztegui, Leopoldo Haces de la Fuente, Teodoro Mayer, Chepe Fortún, Joaquín Prieto, and Agustín Ochoa Mayo, during the inauguration of the Chrysler Distributors Association office facilities.

his activities in the Association and his work with Chrysler and other people who are no longer among us, but who left us indelible memories. His brother Luis, a very dynamic person, worked very closely with him as the President of the State Associations Committee. Jack, his youngest son, also became an outstanding member of our Association."

Some people have often wondered why Wulf Kahan never held the post of President at the AMDA. There are several opinions regarding this matter; some say he did not get the presidency because he never seriously set his mind on it, but there are other people who affirm that he would not have done a good job in giving a speech because of that very special and characteristic accent he had when speaking.

"Don Wulf became very good friends with my father-in-law, Eduardo Orvañanos, who was also in the car dealing business," *says Mr. Christian Schjetnan.* "Don Wulf was a great buddy of his, in part because they both participated at the same time as members of the Board of Directors, and they were both essentially good people; I think that is why they got along so well."

"Don Wulf had some kind of problem with the pronunciation of some letters, and I really never knew why, but it was unthinkable to even mention it around him. He sort of dragged his R's. Despite this problem, he expressed his ideas in a most brilliant manner. Some people say that is the reason why he could not be President of the AMDA; they say they could not imagine having someone give a speech with such a problem, with such a pronunciation."

"He truly loved the Association and worked his back off for it. His only frustration in life, if he ever had one, was the fact of not having been able to serve as AMDA's President. Maybe nobody ever told him, but even though he never made it there, he sure gathered all the qualities to be President."

Don Norberto, who, as I mentioned before, was one of the employees at the Association, says: "Mr. Wulf couldn't become President because of his foreign origin, but boy...he sure would have done one marvelous job!...especially considering all that love he had for the Association."

Don Vicente Ariztegui remembers: "I was really impressed about how beautiful Estela was and how well she spoke English. Wulf did not speak that language, nor was he a perfect Spanish speaker due to the fact that he did not have a good pronunciation. I do not agree with the people that say that this harmed his image at the AMDA. I did support him a lot so he would become President."

"Wulf and I were both members of the Board of Directors at AMDA for a few years, from 1970 to 1973; I was the Association's President and Wulf was the Treasurer," *comments Mr. Alberto Liz.* "When he started his term as Treasurer of the AMDA, his Spanish was not perfect and, because of that, from the first moment he ran across a bit of resistance from the board members, which made him feel a little uncomfortable. Some of the people there did not know him; the ones that worked with Chrysler did, but not the ones working with Ford. Nevertheless, as time passed, everyone grew very fond of him because the man knew how to win their appreciation."

Mr. Jorge Orvañanos also contributes with the following comments:

"My relationship with Wulf started at the AMDA conventions, cocktail parties and work meetings. I also met other people under the same circumstances, like Jorge Garibay, Alberto Liz, Manuel Cortina and Mario Duque, who were all friends with each other."

"I remember a trip we made with several other members of the Board of Directors to a convention held by the American Distributors Association, AMDA's American counterpart. He barely knew how to speak a few words in English back then, but still, he gave various speeches, what caused a very good impression on everyone. How did he do it?...I don't know, but he managed to transmit his ideas and that won him an affectionate ovation from the public and made his participation quite unforgettable."

"As she cracked her fingers, Estela, his wife, was listening to the efforts Wulf made to speak Shakespeare's language. She too, gave her beloved husband a warm and proud round of applause when he finished speaking for she knew better than anyone the hard work he had put into creating his message. The difficulty to express himself in English, or his foreign accent while speaking Spanish, were no obstacles for him."

"I met Wulf Kahan back when his business was located on the streets of Niño Perdido and Río de la Loza," *says Mario Duque,* "and by 1972, I became a member of the Board at AMDA, and then took his place when he left.

He used to always give me good advice; he guided me on two or three occasions when I felt insecure about making a decision. He was a good-hearted man who unselfishly supported the people he knew."

Dr. Miguel Jusidman remembers: "We attended some AMDA reunions with some other car dealers who greeted him with the utmost respect even though they were competitors. He wasn't the kind of man who manipulated a situation to get others to like him, still, everyone highly respected him and it was obvious that they appreciated him as well."

"Wulf Kahan used to attend the board meetings at AMDA, and he continued doing so even after his surgical accident, which seriously limited his physical abilities. Nonetheless," *according to Mr. Alberto López Nava,* "during all the meetings, he would behave in a respectful manner and would try not to get too involved. Yes, he would speak his mind, but he was not the type of person who was constantly interrupting. You could say he had a 'subsidiary' mentality: if he wasn't needed, he would not get involved, but if he was, he would always be there."

Wulf Kahan also participated in the Asociación Mexicana de la Industria Automotriz *(Mexican Association for the Automotive Industry). Mr. César Flores comments:*

"Two years ago, when I became a member of the *AMIA*, I attended a distributors convention for the first time. I did not know very many distributors then and I could not find a place for me to sit at breakfast; when Mr.

Kahan saw me, he invited me to sit at his table. Back then, I had no idea of the identity of the man who was kindly inviting me to share his table, so I dared to ask him who he was. Mr. Kahan told me that the name was not important, what mattered was that we had a good time together. That only proved to me that I had just met a man of great human quality, a man who did not care much about people's status."

In 1990, in the city of Guadalajara, Mr. Diego Garibay gave Wulf Kahan the following letter:

"Today, the Board of Directors of our Association, excepting our President, for obvious reasons which we trust will be understood, has decided to present a humble acknowledgment to a human being who has worked very intensely for our Association, and has always based his actions on the love and respect that characterize all great human beings."

"Since the 1970's and up to this day, with no interruptions or conditions, Wulf Kahan has given the best of himself to our institution. And today, all of us here can do no less than thank you, Wulf, for YOUR EFFORT
YOUR COURAGE
YOUR AFFECTION and
YOUR INTEGRITY,
all of which you show day after day. Thank you for setting an example that teaches us what a true man really is."

"On March 9, 1990, Mr. Ari Kahan was going to take his new position as AMDA's President," *relates Mr. Saul Delgado,* "and that same date was the one scheduled for Don Adolfo's surgery in Houston; so Mr. Ari told him:

'Dad, I'm not going to Huatulco, I'm coming to Houston with you; I want to be there for you during those moments.' And Don Adolfo answered:

'If you don't go to Huatulco and take your place as the new President, I won't have the operation.'

"Being so, Mr. Ari had no choice but to go to Huatulco while Don Adolfo was at a hospital in Houston. I wasn't planning on going to Huatulco, but Don Adolfo told me:

'Saul, go to Huatulco and give Ari the support he needs.' And so I did. I saw Mr. Ari fulfill his duties while his father was in some hospital's surgery room."

"In Huatulco, Ari did not find out about his father's critical state until midnight, the day of his election as AMDA's President; neither his wife Betty, his siblings, Perla, Jack, and Ruth, nor his mom, were willing to ruin that triumphal moment for him. It wasn't until the next morning at dawn, that they flew to Houston to meet Don Wulf."

"During the whole two years of Ari's presidential term at AMDA, Don Wulf never left his son's side; in meetings or during events and lunch reunions. No matter how difficult it was for him, they were always seen together: Don Wulf would always be there showing his unconditional support for Ari."

Wulf Kahan's last appearance in public took place at the AMDA convention in the city of Monterrey, celebrated in 1992. About this, Dr. Sergio Domínguez Vargas has written the following text:

"I had the opportunity of witnessing an incredible case of symbiosis between Don Wulf and his son Ari. Being his last formal appearance as AMDA's President, Ari invited Don Wulf to accompany him to Monterrey."

"Don Wulf accepted the invitation an offered to make an effort to attend the event walking on his own, with his son Jack's help, but without using the wheel chair that had been indispensable to him during his last years of life."

"Maybe it was only a few people who noticed that Don Wulf kept his promise and, while the ceremony was taking place, we saw him walk down the central corridor, almost with no help whatsoever, full of courage and dignity. Ari, his son, had injected him with the strength and will he needed, and which was now shared by them both. In return, Ari felt invaded by a strange tiredness the following day when he went up to the podium and read his last report; that was the completion of the symbiotic cycle with his father, who in those moments was transmitting Ari his weary state of mind."

"That was the last time many of us, his friends, got the opportunity of seeing Don Wulf Kahan alive."

Wulf and Estela Kahan with their children, grandchildren,

CHAPTER VI

The Family:
an Enterprise

Having parents who are respected and appreciated by the society which they form part of, knowing the devotion and love they have for each and everyone of their children, and realizing that the flame of love between them is still alive, is the greatest satisfaction a son could ever experience.

Ari Kahan.

Estela Kahan has always said: "If you want your children near, cook a good meal for them more than once a year." *And she most certainly practiced what she preached. For many years the Kahan's have made it a tradition to gather all around the family table every Friday. Wulf, the patriarch, as someone once called him, was mainly a born businessman: he knew that it is a must to dedicate time and love to one's business. His family was one of Wulf Kahan's greatest enterprises, if not the greatest, and just as with any other enterprise, if you want it to grow, if you want to strengthen the bonds of affection that will make it more powerful, you need to invest in your family. Rolland Bartres used to say that time is man's only real substance and time was precisely one thing Wulf Kahan invested in his family: time and love.*

Arie Derzavich comments that his grandfather "would give us all a weekly allowance every Friday during our lunch reunions, which soon became a tradition in the family. He would do this until one was about thirteen or fourteen years old and I think of it as a really 'neat' thing he used to do, not because of the amount of money that he gave us, but rather because he did it with the knowledge that that way we would always look forward to receiving something from our grandfather; and he did manage to make that something special for all of us: even now, I still remember it as a very nice part of my childhood."

"Going to those family reunions on Fridays is not an obligation for anyone; that is why we enjoy them so much, that is what gives those lunch reunions their true value: we go because we want to, not because we have to. The only thing they do ask from us is that if anyone has other plans and is not coming to one of our gatherings, we just have to tell our grandmother and no problem."

"We all spend some good times together, it doesn't matter whether you are one of the youngest cousins or one of the oldest ones. We all share our experiences and problems with the rest. When any one of us has a problem or is confused about something we all listen to what that person wants to say, and that way, each one gives their own opinion about it, which often proves to be quite helpful. Besides, we know we can talk about anything; there are no restrictions, no scolding anyone about something we say; we all try to help, always, and there's no one better to ask for advice than your own family."

"I recall that during the Friday lunch reunions at my grandfather's place I used to arm wrestle him. I liked it when he put his arms around me and squeezed me very hard. His legs were what amazed me the most about his whole physique: they were extremely strong and hard as rocks."

"He was always very proud about his physical strength; he knew he was a good looking man and he enjoyed it. He would never go unnoticed, not anywhere; his mere presence was imposing. One always felt very safe and comfortable by his side."

During one of the Friday family gatherings, Patty, one of Wulf Kahan's granddaughters, remembers: "I once traveled to Los Angeles with my grandparents. It was a trip in which I felt as if I were traveling with a couple of friends; they spoiled me then like they never had. I became very close to them both and we spent very special moments together. But when Bernardo and I were going to get married everything was different. My grandfather was not very excited about the fact that his granddaughter was marrying someone he did not know, but once he met him, once he got to know him, he learned to love him very much. It was hard for my husband to win him over, but it was worth it. He would always tease me a lot and adored my children -he used to sit them on his lap and tickle them- and my children loved him right back."

Bernardo continues talking about his wife's grandfather: "I lost my father when I was very young; Don Adolfo gave me some advice quite a few times back then and I felt pretty nice about it; I felt him close to me, supporting me, comforting me."

"Being the adventurous person he was, he used to say: 'Nothing ventured, nothing gained.' He liked challenging his grandchildren. When we really got to know each other well, when we learned to trust and love each other, he became a true grandfather to me. I liked to tease him so he would talk. He made an excellent host. I also recall he used to look after his yacht with great care."

"When you become part of the Kahan family, you realize that you will never be alone again. Believe me, I've been there."

Patty and Bernardo's children also had something to tell us. Janisse says that her grandfather, who was actually her great-grandfather: "would always leave saliva on my cheek every time he kissed me and it annoyed me. We sometimes asked him for ice-cream when we were on board the yacht. There was one time we went to a tiny beach, only the two of us, and we ate hamburgers and hot-dogs there. Whenever he looked at me I felt good inside. I love him very much."

Her sister Tali had something to say as well: "We were at his apartment in San Diego one day and I put my *Zeide's*[23] hat on and it made him laugh a lot."

"I had breakfast with him, he gave me lots of kisses, he hugged us very hard and tickled us a lot. We used to have swim races; we played in the water with an inner tube and he used to laugh very much. I miss my Zeide a lot. I always dream about him; I dream that he's on his yacht; he loved being there and we would often go fishing together."

Benjamin, another of his great-grandchildren, son of Heidy and Jorge, relates that his "granddad Wulf was a very special person. He was very fortunate about owning the Chrysler car dealership. I especially remember the time when we went on vacations together on a Princess cruise."

"I also remember clearly the moments when I used to visit him at the hospital during his stay in Houston and from

---

[23] *Yiddish word for grandfather*

his bed he would throw me a ball. I loved my granddaddy Wulf very much."

Following Benjamin's words, his sister Michelle says:

"I remember my granddad sitting in his wheel chair. I recall the times he came to Houston and used to visit us at home. I really enjoyed that time when we all went on a Princess cruise vacation together because I had the chance to play with all my cousins."

"During that vacation trip my granddaddy Wulf would often stand up from his wheel chair and walked with someone's help. I feel sad about the fact that my grandfather Wulf did not have the opportunity to meet my little brother Mark. When my granddaddy died, we left Houston and went down to Mexico and stayed there for seven days."

Michelle is then interrupted by her cousin Alejandro who adds: "He used to play with me very often and mischievously teased me a lot; we used to go swimming together in the pool he had at home. He always joked around with me quite a bit. I loved him very much and he said he loved me, too; he told me that many times. He also used to take me to McDonald's, which I thought was very nice."

The thoughts of his older grandchildren show that they did try to make the best use of the advice they got from Wulf Kahan and, most of all, they prove that through time they learned to enjoy his presence much more.

Carlos says: "I must have been about seventeen years old when I started working at the dealership; the last thing I wanted then was to be anywhere near my grandfather. He was very strict when it came to following a schedule and regarding the quality of somebody's work. However, in the future I was able to establish my own business, that is, the first Domino's Pizza franchises in Mexico, and I took him to see the site where I was going to open the first of these pizza places. After checking the place out, just a few minutes after we had arrived there, he told me:

'You are going to have problems in the long run if you establish your business here.' But I didn't want to listen to what I thought was an exaggeration on his part for my grandfather had not examined the whole site thoroughly when he said that. Unluckily for me, he had been right about everything, everything he had told me then but it took me a year to realize it. I was able to notice that only after the problems had already started."

"I clearly remember that once, when I was working at his company, he appointed me to make out an inventory of all the vehicles that were being repaired in the workshop at the time. I did a thorough job on it and when I was done I gave him a report on the inventory; he took a quick look at it and, almost immediately, he said:

'There are cars missing in this report.'
'No, there aren't,' I said, 'they are all there.'
'Let's go see,' he told me and we went down to the workshop."

"He walked around the workshop and he proved to me that, in fact, there were some cars that I had not included in the inventory lists. It was amazing how sharply and quickly his mind worked."

"One time, my father, my brother Saul, my grandmother, him and I were all on the yacht traveling from Acapulco to Ixtapa. It was a great trip. He taught us how to actually control the yacht, how to leave the docks, and how to bring the yacht in. He liked to joke around blowing the whistle when we were not paying attention or when we were taking a nap on deck while we sunbathed, and he would laugh at the way we reacted when that caught us by surprise."

"Breakfast would be served always at the same hour: seven o'clock, and we all had to be there. No one could sleep in, no matter how late we had gone to bed the night before."

"Once, he woke me up very early in the morning and he already had everything prepared so we could go fishing; it was only going to be him and me. That time we only caught one fish, which he cooked later and we had it for lunch."

"I enjoyed cooking his favorite dish for him while we were on board: fried bacon and onions -very fried. He didn't mind if the yacht got impregnated with the smell or if my grandma worried about him eating that; she said it was not healthy for him because of the high amount of fat in it."

Saul treasures many memories which he expresses as though he were chatting face to face with his grandfather:

"It was you, remember granddad, who gave me the keys to my first car as you said that the ones after those, I would have to pay for myself. Then you got into the car with me and we went for a ride, me at the driver's seat. Boy, you really did trust your young grandson!"

"It was also you who taught me the basic principles on which I now run my professional career... 'if you want things to get done right, first you have to set an example, yourself,' you said."

"I believe that when you reprimanded me -always with a touch of affection- about arriving late to work, it was one of the many ways of showing just how much you loved me and how important it was for you to teach me the bases and foundations that a working man must follow."

"How could I ever forget that morning, back in 1983, when I told you I was leaving the family business to start my own... 'So that is what I worked for during more than 60 years, so you can leave and not continue with the family tradition started by your great-grandfather, my father, who you were named after.' You came down on me so hard that day. Nor will I forget that feeling, so great, when I heard you say a few years later what you would repeat so many times, often with words, other times with actions, and some others with just a simple look, a hug, a strong handshake, a joke: that is the way you showed me how proud you felt about what I had accomplished. Granddad, I was only following your footsteps."

"The relationship you and I had, dear granddad, has left its mark deep inside my soul. Perhaps a lot of what I have done in my life and what I will do is and will be a reflection of the things you taught me."

"All those moments and experiences...the trip to Laredo... 'Grandfather, let me drive'... 'No, I can do it. I know this highway like the palm of my hand. Do you even know how many times I have traveled to and from Detroit on this road?' You drove for almost eighteen hours straight; and you would have kept on going if it hadn't been for that torn engine belt. And we waited until the next morning to go find a new belt which you would put back on the engine all on your own. Nothing ever stopped you."

"One day in Acapulco... 'Granddad, where did you and grandma go last night?'

'We went to the Bocaccio. Look, here I have the photos...we danced all night long.' Wow!, I thought, you made such a great couple. You had already started to grow some gray hair and you still loved to go dancing and stay out until dawn."

"But what about the times it was me who stayed out late...
'Saul, wake up, we have to go buy the groceries for the yacht.'
'But granddad, I just got here.'
'Well, you'll just have to wait until tonight to get your sleep,' you would say."

Jackie, Perla's son affirms that:

"I admired the way my grandfather led his life. He always fought hard to obtain all what he possessed. His eyes, his look...it was very strong, very explosive; whenever he was happy, one could see a very special glow in his eyes. His main goal was living and enjoying life to the fullest."

"During all parties, he liked walking around and meeting people, he danced...he just wouldn't stay in his seat. He was the life of the party at Carlos' wedding. He slipped while he was dancing with the bride and we all thought he had hurt himself, but he immediately got up again as if nothing had happened. He was 75 years old and he kept on dancing."

"One time, I had invited some friends over to Acapulco, but there were already a lot of guests staying at our place and I felt offended for we didn't have any more space to fit my friends in. I spent that whole night wondering why he had done that to me. The next day at breakfast I told my grandfather I was upset about what had happened but he talked to me in private, just him and me, and explained himself in such a way that I finally understood the situation. I cried and we hugged."

"I think I am a lot like him when it comes to expressing my feelings with words. He expressed his love for someone by dedicating time to the relationship, giving advice, paying attention, caring about that person."

"He considered all the problems we talked to him about very important; he really cared for others. He gave so much to everyone, but mostly to his family."

"He enjoyed every gift he gave; giving was his greatest satisfaction. Giving was a motive of pride, satisfaction, and happiness for him. Grandparents sometimes give you a present so they'll get a kiss from you in return, or something of that sort. With him it was the other way around. His hands were a reflection of his life: on the back they were soft and his palms were all rough. In Acapulco he would get so involved in fixing the yacht's engine and if he noticed that his car had some kind of problem he would fix it himself; he would not wait for anyone to carry things for him, he would pick up almost anything, he did everything on his own. Many times I even saw him checking cars in the workshop back at the dealership."

"He was a man of actions rather than words; he even did some house work when the maid was out on her day off. It didn't really matter to him if he got his hands all dirty and greasy when he had to replace a light bulb or do that kind of things. Before falling ill, he was the one who drove his car, not the chauffeur; he would only accompany him and park the car and wait for him when they went somewhere. He never liked to depend on anybody; I believe that this was the reason why he couldn't overcome his illness."

"He was an extremely independent man and any other situation was unacceptable to him. His death represents a great loss. I will always remember him; his image will stay with me forever."

Samy, Jackie's brother, also talks about his grandfather:

"He was a person with a lot of self-confidence; he knew how to treat people right, he knew a lot of people, he made many friends, and was a giving and loving human being. I remember I was riding in his car -a Chrysler Phantom- one day and I felt very proud and safe having him on the driver's seat. He had amazing convincing powers."

"He supported us all the time; he was the center of the family, he always knew how to keep things under control, and he was a friend to us all."

"I remember one of my grandfather's birthday celebrations that took place at my uncle Antonio's ranch. There, I asked him if he was truly happy with who he was and what he had, and he answered: 'Of course I am happy, I'm a person who has a wife, children, grandchildren...there's no greater happiness than that.' I believe he was very wise. I would like to be like him when I grow older and be surrounded by people who love me."

Wulf Kahan's grandchildren continue talking about their grandfather as they interrupt one another; each of them has an experience to tell, each a different anecdote, however, they all have one thing in common: the love they felt for their granddad.

"For my parents' 25th wedding anniversary," *says Anna,* "we all took a trip together to Europe and I remember that all through the trip there was a Spanish family that would always sit near us and on the exact day of the anniversary you, granddad, started dancing and singing as you played the maracas."

"Watching the look on your face when we arrived in Russia, I could only imagine all the things that were going through your mind and I felt proud as you went on telling us about experiences you barely remembered. You used to tell me something that made me very happy and is still fresh in my mind, and up to this day I always repeat it wearing a smile on my face: '*chutnaya dziebechka*' which means 'pretty girl'."

"If I could only turn back time and relive those marvelous moments we all shared with my Zeide, a full-fledged captain. I cherish the trips we made to San Diego in which I used to sleep in the guest room or in the family room and you -I don't know why- always made noise all around the place. You could not stand the sight of anyone still being asleep passed eight o'clock in the morning and I would get upset about that all the time; nevertheless, I still enjoyed those moments very much. I often told you how amazed I was about how strong and well-shaped your legs were."

"The path you followed during your life, granddaddy, has taught me a lot: you were a man who fought hard to achieve what he wanted, as an entrepreneur, as a friend, as a companion, as a father, as a grandfather, and much more; a man who earned the obedience of many people. You managed to make people respect you, not fear you, because we knew that you were a person with a great heart, incapable of harming anyone."

"Granddaddy, now that I am about to marry David and form my own family, I pray to God that He grant me a life and a family like the one you created, respectful and loving, but most of all, I pray that I have the fortune of forming a happy couple; you and my grandma have been my greatest example: together for 55 years, loving and respecting each other, being friends to one another, sharing every moment, good and bad, but always together."

"You know? I would give anything if only I could have you by my side so I could learn more from you, because there was so much more in you I never knew...but although you are not here physically, I know and I feel you are with me in every step I take, in every decision I make, you're right there giving me your opinion and encouraging me to go on with my life."

"Thank you, granddad, for being my granddaddy."

Right after Anna's words, Sandra remembers that she "saw him as an elegant, handsome, young prince, whose eyes shimmered as if everything was made of gold; for him, everything had an immeasurable value and that is why all that surrounded him made him incredibly happy. Ever since I was a little girl I would get very excited whenever he went to pick us up at the airport in Acapulco. It was such a joy for me to know everyone was watching me holding the hand of the most handsome young man in the world. But he impressed me all the time because I would show off his elegance and still, he wouldn't take advantage of that crown I imagined on his head and treated everybody else with respect and courtesy."

"He was just like a bag full of tricks. My grandma used to say that he had the same mischievous expression on his face like the one all his grandchildren had when they were about to pull a prank on someone. He was part of our team; it was him, my cousins, my brothers and me against the adults' strict mentality. He always had some idea to contribute to our pranks and he helped us carry them out since he obviously had better access to the grown-up world than the rest of us scoundrels all together."

"I considered him the most intrepid adventurer in the world. He loved speed and I must admit that, even though I liked riding with him, once every now and then my face, as well as other people's who were also in the car, would reflect a fearful expression. But somehow, I felt reassured knowing that he was an excellent captain and one of the best car pilots, and that nothing could ever happen to me as long as I was with him. I recall my grandma screaming every time he drove the car over the speed limit: 'Adolfo, I'm telling you to slow down! Adolfo, you're going to scare the poor kids!' And he would have that mischievous expression on his face when he turned his head around to see her. He would then tell her that he loved her and, noticing that the 'kids' were splitting their sides laughing, he would keep on driving at full speed."

"I also remember him as being a fantastic businessman. His company has exceptional prestige and, therefore, being the leader of such enterprise, he was very pressured. He knew, however, how to face things and who to deal with, and he never showed his worries in front of the family. His employees had great respect for him, not only because he was their boss, but because they loved him, as well. He gave a personal treatment to all the people who ever got involved in his business; his quality as a leader is more noticeable in the way the employees express themselves about him, rather than in the company's numbers. I consider him to be one of the best friends I have ever had. He understood me almost without me having to say a word and helped me without having the need to ask him to. We could spend hours enjoying each other's company; I loved simply being around him. As long as he was near, there would always be something for me to do: boredom did not exist when he was there. In Acapulco, waking up in the mornings due to his yelling was actually quite invigorating. When I woke up at ridiculously early hours, he was already set and waiting for us to go swimming. One of my clearest memories is about one night that he and I went swimming and played in the pool like a couple of little kids. We spent hours playing and watching the stars as if neither time nor age existed and almost without speaking we understood each other perfectly. It was as though he knew exactly what my qualities and my tastes were without me having to knowingly show them to him."

"I remember him as a love genius: he loved and was loved by everyone who knew him. He was a person who knew what his mission in life was and he carried it out until the last moment. He was able to show everybody that loving and being loved is a natural thing and he led his life sticking to that thought. Now, I want to thank God for having given me the opportunity of sharing fifteen years of my life with him. And there is just one thing left for me to tell my Zeide: I will love you forever."

The importance that Wulf Kahan gave to each person as an individual is an outstanding characteristic that all these comments have in common. Even though he had a very numerous family, every one of its members had his or her special place in the family. Given the context, Irene affirms that she "felt loved by him, not only as his grandson's wife, but more as a person. He was a very open minded, very cheerful man; one could talk about anything with him. He wasn't old fashioned at all; what's even more, he grew as a person with every day that went by."

"I believe my future life by Saul's side, when we grow old, will be similar to the one my husband's grandparents led. I would truly like that; they got along very well, they loved each other immensely; as a couple, they knew the real meaning of enjoying their children, their grandchildren, their great-grandchildren, their wealth, and most of all, when it came to sharing things with others, they knew how to do it on a grand scale. When my husband, Saul, decided to leave the car dealing business to start his own McDonald's franchise business, Don Adolfo said at first that he couldn't believe that a family tradition was being broken and some other things regarding that; nevertheless, with time, he learned to accept the decision he had taken, he learned to respect it and support it."

Mossy tells us:

"Talking about a person whose existence left an enormous trace in the hearts of so many people, isn't easy at all. Yes, I'm referring to him, to his memory, to a model human being. I did not have much time to get to know him, but it was enough for me to learn a lot from him only by observing the way he acted."

"I don't feel it is necessary to describe all the beautiful things that made that great man who he was. If he could be with us again, even if it were only for a few instants, the only thing I would ask from him would be for him to dedicate some time to his great-grandson, that little person who never got the chance of meeting him. That is one thing that is very painful for me, it hurts a lot; however, at the same time, I have a great feeling of satisfaction just for the fact that he was named after his great-granddad; a very special name, a very special person."

"I believe that having his great-grandfather's name, little Adolfo definitely represents the completion of a chain of generations."

There are different points of view and a great diversity of opinions expressed in the thoughts of Wulf Kahan's grandchildren; all of them contribute to the creation of that very dear image of him which they treasure. For example, Daniel's memories are more playful, more cheerful:

"I remember he loved cars, boats, and speed; these were his three favorite things in life. He was a happy man and liked practicing sports, as well. He used to gladly pinch our cheeks whenever he saw us; it was kind of painful, but he loved doing it."

"One day, Jaime, Arie, my dad, my Zeide, and I went fishing. We stayed out there for hours and hours until we finally caught a fish; we were all very excited, but also very tired and burnt by the sun. I also remember seeing him on the beach, in Acapulco, lying under the shade and chatting. He was always chatting with everyone. That is how I realized that everybody liked him."

Gabriel also talks about Acapulco, the yacht, and the sea, Wulf Kahan's three most favorite topics:

"My Zeide was not only my granddaddy, he was my friend, too. I remember the great moments we spent together."

"He was a sweet person; I always saw him with a smile and in a happy mood. Every time I think of him, it reminds me of Acapulco. He taught me how to water-ski there and he would stand on the highest part of his yacht and dive off into the sea."

"He invited me to go fishing with him one day: It was six in the morning and when he came to wake me up he had already taken a shower and was all set to go. When we left the apartment, my hair was a terrible mess and I was still half asleep, and he would crack up laughing every time he turned around to see me because of the way I looked and how sleepy I was."

"That day I felt quite seasick on board the yacht and I threw up for having fallen asleep in a cabin below deck. I also recall the moments when we used to have breakfast together and he'd tell us about his life back in Russia and how he had left the country. Once in a while, he would let me smoke his pipe when we went to San Diego; I liked it."

Then Katiana chats with her grandfather:

"I'm one of your youngest granddaughters, but I would have liked to have more time to spend with you and experience the nice and happy moments you lived with my aunts and uncles, with my cousins, and especially with my *Babbi*[24] and my dad."

"I was very young back then, when you hadn't had your operation yet, but still, I remember some things like the times in Acapulco when I woke up in the mornings an I found that you had already gone swimming, you had taken a shower, and you were ready to take us all to the yacht."

"When you passed away, my aunt Ruthy told us your life story and it made me think: my granddad had gone from poverty to wealth and was the happiest man ever for having married the greatest woman: my Babbi. Then I realized that my granddaddy had been the best."

And Alexander, the youngest of all his grandchildren, says:

"What I remember the most about my Zeide Wulf is the times that we went to Miami and at night we would go to the cinema. I would always sit beside him. I also remember that whenever I went to his house, I used to sit on his lap when he was sitting in his wheel chair and Fernando would take us for a 'ride'. We talked and he would always laugh when he saw me arrive at his house. I miss him and love him a lot."

[24] *Grandmother*

Gabriela adds that her grandfather "would wake us up very early in the mornings to go swimming. He was always very active and in the mood for playing with us. He was like a kid who never wanted to grow up. His yacht was his favorite diversion. He would wear his captain's hat and would stand by the steering wheel, feeling the air against his face and with his beautiful hair blown back with the wind. I recall he once took us to watch the dolphins swimming by on one side of the yacht; we felt afraid, but he said in a tender voice: everything's all right."

For one reason or another, Wulf's image always left a positive mark, a happy, lively, pleasant memory.

"In my mind, I have this image of my grandfather surrounded by people all the time," *says Heidy.* "He was always with people: wherever he went you would find him with someone, he was never alone. He was a man with a lot of charisma who would always become the center of everyone's attention wherever he was. He made everyone around him feel good."

"I remember that once, I went on a trip to Los Angeles with my grandparents. My grandma and I would go shopping. I love to shop and one time we went to the mall and stayed there almost the entire day. When we went back home that day, my grandfather said he wanted to go out and he took us to see a *Cantinflas* movie. Besides liking his films because he was one of the best Mexican comedians, he felt something special for him because he was his neighbor in Los Angeles, where he had his apartment, and also, the car dealership he had on Ejercito Nacional had been used as a location to shoot one of the scenes in that specific Cantinflas film. My grandmother and I liked it very much, but he...he was extremely excited about having seen his dealership on the silver screen."

From Israel, Jaime sends the following text about his Zeide:

"Now that I am here, in direct contact with my roots and my religion, I have developed more of an ability to express my feelings about a person who throughout his whole life was always so close to God."

"He was a man who loved life like no one I have ever known. Being by his side meant living beautiful experiences. His yacht...we enjoyed his yacht so much. He liked scaring everyone by making it go at full speed. I liked going for a ride with him on his small fishing boat; he used to laugh a lot when we soared over the waves. When I was a little kid I felt that it was going to send me flying through the air. We had a very fun time together. I also liked to go water-skiing with him...I felt him more as one of my best friends, rather than just my grandfather. He never was the age he claimed to be, he was young, he was always our age."

"I remember him being strong as an oak and always very active. We liked to arm wrestle each other but I could never beat him at it. If we were all at a party, he loved challenging us to see who could drink the most and, of course, my cousins and I could never keep up with him."

"I feel that my Zeide, besides leaving me a lot of nice memories, left me good examples for me to follow: his love for his wife, for his children, for his children-in-law, for us, his grandchildren and great-grandchildren. I recall it was incredibly easy for him to make new friends, no matter their origins; everyone loved him. Wherever he went, the people there knew him. I admire his honesty, his way of living; he spent his best moments with my Babbi."

"I remember the day my mom called me into her room and when I entered, I saw her crying; she wanted to let me know that my father and she were going to travel to Houston because my Zeide was going to have an operation. I hugged her and asked her not to cry anymore. I told her that my Zeide was not going to let an operation bring him down. And he didn't; he fought until the last moment of his life, showing courage while he confronted all the adversities."

"Zeide, I will live eternally grateful for the many wonderful moments I enjoyed by your side, and I thank you for all that you taught me."

On the other hand, Arie summarizes, in a few words, the importance of his grandfather's family name:

"It's because of him that I believe that Kahan is much more than a simple family last name; it is an attitude towards life that exists within each one of our individual personalities; of course, no one has the obligation of being this or that way, but every one of us is a 'Kahan' in his or her own special way."

Fernando Derzavich, husband of Perla, Wulf Kahan's oldest daughter, remembers:

"My father-in-law, a person who lived his life so intensely, who enjoyed every moment of it, showed us that he did not consider money as being first on his list; he did not hoard it, on the contrary, he knew how to enjoy it: he bought his very first yacht, the SEA WULF I, his house on the street of Prado, and later, the apartment at the Playasol building, in Acapulco, the one in Century City, in Los Angeles, and a whole bunch of other things."

"Ever since I met him, since 1960, when I got married to Perlita, he led his life that way. We spent the summer vacations with him and enjoyed part of that energy with which he lived. He would never let us sleep until late for he already had a whole fun-filled day planned out: golf, fishing, Pichilingue beach, water-skiing, lunch, etc."

"He helped me in several occasions: in 1990, when I had a terrible problem with the worker's union, he was greatly concerned and asked his friend Federico Anaya Sánchez to help me find a solution. On another occasion, when my son Jackie had an accident with an exhibition balloon that exploded and there were a lot of people injured because of it, he, once more, offered us his help to solve the problem. To other people, this may seem a normal thing to do but, unfortunately, my father-in-law was already ill and this makes his actions in this respect much more valuable to me."

The other one of Wulf Kahan's two sons-in-law, José Gancz, tells us that:

"The relationship between my father-in-law and me started off in the worst way possible: I was in Acapulco and I had invited Ruthy to lunch the day after we met because we had gotten along very well. Ruthy told me that she had already planned to go out to lunch with her parents, but that, surely, there would be no problem if I wanted to come along. So I did. We arrived at the restaurant Beto's, a place on the beach, and as we sat down, we noticed that they were shooting a beer commercial on the beach right next to the restaurant. My father-in-law, with that very special way he had of stereotyping people, immediately said that 'all people in the advertising business are either alcoholics or drug addicts' and Ruthy and I, without saying a word, just looked at each other because I was in charge of the advertising department at Procter and Gamble. A few minutes later, he asked me what I did for a living and when I told him what my job was, all of a sudden, there was a sepulchral silence at the table; then, my mother-in-law, very gracefully, started talking about a whole other subject. I still believe that during that brief moment of silence my father-in-law was trying to figure out whether the boy accompanying his daughter was a drug addict, or simply a drunk."

"Ever since that very tough experience, the relationship between Don Adolfo and me got better and better until the day he passed away. We developed a relationship based on mutual respect, affection, and created a friendship so strong, that my greatest wish in life is that

I may one day have that same type of relationship with my sons-in-law."

Wulf not only loved, but also had deep respect for Betty, one of his daughters-in-law. They were both people of very strong character and, more often than not, they tried to get their way. The disputes they had were all rich in arguments but after too much discussing they would finally reach an agreement.

The slightest provocation would always become the best excuse to start this: everything from deciding which restaurant to go to, to planning a trip. They argued quite often because of the most insignificant things; even about which way to take to get from one place to another, which road had less traffic lights. Nevertheless, they appreciated each other very much. Thanks to Betty's perseverance, in spite of Wulf's illness, we were able to make the trip in which we celebrated Wulf and Estela's 55th wedding anniversary. The entire Kahan family acknowledges Betty's professional skills as a travel agent and in organizing that unforgettable event. Wulf always admired his daughter-in-law's intelligence and her extraordinary human quality. "I doubt my Ari could ever find a better companion than Betty," he used to say.

Tita, Jackie's wife, dedicates a few words to her father-in-law:

"To my dearest Don Wulf:

Writing just one anecdote would be too unfair when

Estela and Wulf Kahan's gold wedding anniversary.

one wants to describe fifteen years of both beautiful and sad experiences in one's life.

I had the honor of knowing the fighter, the optimistic person, the man, the father, the grandfather, and especially, the friend that you were. Small would be the amount of words that could describe you, but they would express an enormous amount of feelings.

When I think of you, I think about success, I think about life, and I don't let myself fall so easily; I simply have to remind myself that you held on to life and challenged death until your last moment. Don Wulf, this is the only way I can think of expressing my gratitude, my admiration, my love, and how much I miss you.

May God bless you."

In the next paragraphs, Perla, Wulf Kahan's oldest daughter, describes some of her memories:

"He was a divine father. I think his friendship towards us, his complete dedication to us, his gentle ways, they are all gone and I feel terribly empty inside. He always had a loving embrace for his family; I miss him so much."

"During my teenage years, I was always free to do whatever I pleased; I could count on his understanding all the time, on his advice, and especially on his trust. He would always have an attentive ear when it came to my needs, he always encouraged me to do what I believed was right; he would tell us: Don't you worry, just do what you consider is right and everything will turn out fine."

"He loved to dance, and as a matter of fact, he was an excellent dancer. He was also a jealous father but, in spite of that, he would never limit us in any way. When he hugged us, he would do it in an honest, open, strong way."

"There was one occasion that I went to a convention on behalf of my mom, who was pregnant with my brother Jack at the time. I attended the convention with my dad and I felt as if I were 'queen for a day'; it was fabulous. I'll never forget that moment."

"My parents would 'abandon' us to go to the conventions and I would be left in charge of running the house and taking care of my brothers and my sister; that made me feel more responsible."

"I was a child who often threw temper tantrums. Once, we made a trip to Ixtapan de la Sal and that was the first time my dad ever spanked me because I didn't want to let my mom brush my hair. I had gotten really out of control and there was no other way of making me calm down. Of course, that was a terrible experience for me; he had never done anything like that before; it was my mom who had the heavy hand in the family. That was the only time he ever hit me."

"My mom was my dad's advisor when it came to clothing. Sometimes she even caught him already in the elevator leaving for work and sent him back to change his clothes for some other outfit that would combine better, and he would tell her:

'But, sweetheart, it looks fine.'
Then my mom would answer:
'There is no way I am letting you leave this house dressed like that. You are going to the office and you must look good.'

And he was always very clean, always well shaved, and always nicely dressed."

"Anita, my grandmother on my father's side, who was very strict, worked with my grandfather in his business; it was both of them side by side. When the economic situation got better, she no longer had to work in the family business and devoted herself to helping the needy and doing acts of charity. My grandfather was an observant of the Jewish traditions; although he wasn't very religious, he did observe the Jewish festivities."

"My father had a Dodge car dealership and when we were kids he used to pick us up at school in a motorcycle he had; we would feel like a million bucks riding with him. They called him *Gaucho Veloz*[25]. Speed was always one of his greatest passions; no matter if it was on a motorcycle, a car, a boat, or any other vehicle, he loved the feeling of going fast. He did not compete in the Pan-American Race only because we did not let him, because we were afraid that something could happen to him. But if it had been

---

[25] *Speeding 'gaucho'. A gaucho is an Argentinian expert horseman or cowboy.*

only up to him, he would have done it, for sure. He never missed a car race, although it was just as a spectator."

"My father never resigned himself to his illness; he fought hard against it, never sat back and let it be. He gave up only after attending the convention in Monterrey, after having made such an enormous effort to be there. I believe that that was when he lowered the curtain, in that exact moment, because he said: 'I kept my promise, I walked to Monterrey.' His dignity was hurt from the moment in which he had to depend on his wheel chair."

"He left us beautiful memories; he was a person who frequently spoke well about everything; his way of speaking was very effective. I don't recall anyone ever having a complaint about him. I would like my children to have the same opinions about me one day as the ones my siblings and I have about my parents."

"The most admirable thing about him is that even without a scholar education, he made it to the very top. He did not feel intimidated by the fact that he had no academic education."

Last, but not least, Ruthy, Wulf's youngest daughter, has sent the following text from the city of Torreón:

"It's easy to speak about how great a man Wulf Kahan was because he was a person who had a thousand beautiful, profound, and sometimes funny sides to his personality; nevertheless, thinking of the great loss it was for me, talking about him is very difficult."

"First of all, I must say that he was an excellent father in every sense; he was never too busy or too tired, he would never say 'I can't talk to you right now, we'll do it tomorrow.' He always had time to listen, no matter if it was only a child's trifle or if it concerned a serious problem when we became adults. HE WAS MY GREAT FRIEND."

"It doesn't take a lot of effort on my part for my memories of him to constantly pop into my mind. I remember him whenever I look at the sea, one of his greatest passions; he used to take us swimming when we were children and if I said that the water was too cold or if I felt afraid about going in, he would give me the courage I needed by saying: 'There, there, sweetheart, it's all right,' and that was the way he helped me understand that there was no such thing for him as saying 'I can't'."

"I remember him when I look at the way the city is decorated with lights during the national holidays, during Christmas time; the decorations on the Angel of Independence, all along Reforma Avenue, in Chapultepec Park, and all those other streets along which he used to drive us when we were kids. He was indefatigable. He could not stand being at home for too long and he really enjoyed taking us for 'a ride', as he used to call it. He would get in the car and would drive around for hours, with no set direction, all of us together, him at the wheel...That's how he lived his life: HIM AT THE WHEEL."

"I also remember him whenever I see a swimming pool; I recall how he cried his eyes out with laughter when we fell into the water every time he pushed us in. That's right, if we were standing anywhere around the pool, distracted, he would just come up to us and push us right into the water. Once we had gotten over the scare, we turned to see him and he would be there, crying with laughter. He never stopped being a mischievous little boy."

"I recall that the time we took a trip on a cruise in the Caribbean, we were assigned to a cabin which was barely big enough for all of us. It was practically impossible for four people to sleep in there: it was my mom, my dad, Jackie, and me. Since my dad and I suffer from claustrophobia, we were forced to make a decision and ended up sleeping out on deck. It was a very nice experience for we were able to spend a lot of time chatting and it all felt very peaceful; the breeze and the waves were lullabying us to sleep and he was there, right by my side, making sure that nothing happened to me."

"I also recall the day Pepe went to ask my parents for my hand in marriage. My mom had come up with a whole plan because we knew that my dad was not going to make things very easy, not because he had something against Pepe, but because it was actually going to be very difficult for him to give anyone my hand in marriage. Well, even with a plan and all, he didn't accept that time. Then came the second try and again he said no. It had nothing to do with my fiancé, it was just the fact that it meant I was going to start a whole new life of my own away from them for I was going to move to Torreón. The third time that Pepe went to my father, he then had no choice but to accept because he knew that it was the decision I had made for myself. My wedding day was the happiest day of my entire life for I was beginning a new life with the man I love the most; nevertheless, it was also the saddest moment because that meant that I was no longer going to be able to enjoy my dad, my mom, and my siblings as I had done until then. I would only have them with me once every now and then, or I would just speak to them on the phone. It was a very tough decision for me to make."

"If he was invited to a wedding ceremony on a Sunday, I remember he would come home after the reception with a bunch of people and would continue the party there. And my mom, being the good hostess that she is, even that late at night, would prepare some eggs and some sausage and many other things to serve as breakfast for all the people my dad had invited over. My mother was always the great woman behind that great man."

"He had an armchair he loved to sit on whenever he came to visit me at home. He used to sit there and read the paper after having gone for his daily walk with mom. They were both very elegant dressers: even if they were only wearing sweats, they always looked very sophisticated. That armchair, now that he is no longer alive, has helped me talk to him when I have felt overcome by sadness. I don't recall him ever saying 'I'm too tired, we'll talk tomorrow;' I know I can come to that chair any time and he will be there, listening to me. I sometimes go outside and turn my head to see the sky and I know that, from up there, he still spends many hours chatting with me; he is still guiding me, just as he did when I could still hear his voice. Sometimes it is as if I could hear him say 'it's all right, darling, it's all right,' in that sweetest voice I will forever remember."

"When he and mom decided to buy the apartment in San Diego, they came to us with the suggestion that we buy one of our own in that same building. It was a great opportunity to spend our summer vacations together, to share incredible times for two whole months every year. So we bought the apartment and it turned out to be a place of many beautiful experiences. Every time my children left for summer day camp, my parents would be standing out on their balcony, waving good-bye and wishing them a wonderful day. When they came back in the afternoons, their grandparents would be waiting there to take them out somewhere. Those were the two months of the year we would all look forward to the most every year."

"I remember him being impeccably dressed all the time, with that grace that characterized him, his hair neatly combed, his smile, his personal charm...all that made me very proud whenever I walked with him arm in arm. My dad would be the best dancer at every party we went to. I loved dancing with him. He used to be the soul of all parties and reunions. There was nothing impossible for him; he believed that everything could be done as long as one really set one's heart on it, and that was one of his legacies to his family: his honesty, his charitable nature. I could go on and on just mentioning the very many qualities he, a great man in every sense of the word, had."

"I always think of him when I'm at work because after he fell ill I was determined to make myself understand what had caused him to end up that way. I was so shocked by what had happened that I decided to find out first what it was that he was feeling; and so, with my husband's and my children's wonderful support, I went to Houston, where I studied to become a speech therapist, specializing in treating people who, like my dad, had suffered a stroke. That way, I was able to understand the terrible things he was going through. Due to the fact that I lived too far away for me to be of any help to his illness, I offered my help to other people back home who were going through the same problems he was."

"I felt that, although I was far from him physically, I was somehow helping him by treating my patients. Now that he is gone, I am working in honor of his memory and helping those people to achieve a better quality of life until God decides against it."

"I recall the last time I spoke with my dad: I had called to thank him for the sculpture he and mom had sent us for our 25th wedding anniversary. I told him where I was going to place it, he agreed and started crying, as if he were saying good-bye. He remembered that it had been 25 years ago when I had decided to move far away from them. His last words to me were: 'YOU ARE SO FAR AWAY, SWEETHEART.' Six days after that, while I was in a therapy session, I received a phone call from Mexico City in which I was told that my dad had passed away."

"When I talked to him for the last time, he promised me that, no matter what, he was going to be with us on our anniversary. God no longer let him live to be with us then, but my mom, my sister, my brothers, my in-laws, and my nephews and nieces, they all agreed that if he had made that promise to me, they were going to keep it for him and came up to spend that very special day with us. It had been barely three weeks since my father's death when they all traveled to Torreón to be with Pepe, my children, and me on such an important occasion. My dad was there, as well; present within each one of us, injecting us with his smile, even though we weren't in the mood for smiling much. Thank you, my family. We will never forget that."

"His memory will live in my heart and the hearts of all the people who knew him. REST IN PEACE, MY FRIEND WULF."

Wulf Kahan in Acapulco.

CHAPTER VII

A Man

The man who lives the most is not the one who lives the longest, but he who wastes the least days in his lifetime.

Anonymous.

The thing to catch the most is this lifestyle
who you are but you can't but it's the worst that
lives here is his life no.

"Adolfo and I found that we had been born on the same day and year and that made us develop a much closer bond between us; we were like brothers," *says Dr. Fernando Katz,* "we were both immigrants and, although I had become a doctor and he had taken an interest in business, my relationship with him remained something very special, very close, very dear."

Undoubtedly, friendship was one of the most valuable things in life for Wulf Kahan; his personal charm helped him keep a relationship with his friends throughout his entire life.

Another one of Wulf Kahan's main characteristics in his personality was his cheerfulness. His restless nature was always on the look out and ready to enjoy life constantly: everything from the smallest details to the most magnificent events. The smile that dressed his face could easily disappear if the situation called for it; then, he would become strict and sometimes even tough. But, especially, his joy and ability to appreciate the most insignificant moments in life made it possible for Wulf Kahan to establish intense and affectionate bonds with people much younger than him, whether they were members of the family or just friends, and for his influence to leave a mark in all their lives.

Mr. Ben Schoenfeld comments on this aspect of Wulf Kahan's life:

"The image I have of him is one of a true patriarch and of a great leader within his enterprise. I really enjoyed listening to him and being with him for he was a very experienced man and all that he commented would always prove to be extremely useful to the young people."

Mr. Fernando Cohen also says:

"Despite the difference in age between us, we always got along very well. Mr. Kahan could sometimes be a very tough man but, most of all, he was a great father to his children. I considered him to be like a second father to me; he even expected me to greet him every time with a hug and a kiss."

"He was a man who had an immense experience in the branch of automotive business, since he was one of the industry's pioneers in Mexico," *adds Mr. Carlos Kretchmer.* "He knew how to manage his time. I have no idea of how he administered the hours of the day, but he always had the time to take care of his clients. In this business, one could learn a lot from his experience just by chatting with him. He was always willing to help the young people learn as much as possible from what he could say to us."

According to the opinion given by Arie Derzavich, Wulf's grandson, his grandfather's influence on him played a decisive role in the achievement of his goals:

"As a matter of fact, I believe that even having the 'drive' to accomplish things in life is something that others inculcate in you; at least in my case, I think it was. Or perhaps, it was something I learned; but one thing I am sure of is that my grandfather's way of leading his life had a great influence on me. I feel that I learned to be the way that I am from knowing his life story and becoming aware of his drive, his desire to solve any problem. He considered it was a must to solve a problem and do it at the precise moment, not one minute later. I believe that every goal he reached was a problem solved; that's the way he was. In my mind I hold a very strong image of my grandfather, which I think will prove very helpful throughout my entire life. He used to say 'where there's a will, there's a way'; if you really wanted something, you had to fight for it, you had to work hard for it; that was the secret to success, and you had to keep your mind running, you had to be creative."

"Wulf Kahan was quite a few years older than me," *says Mr. Gilberto Cantú.* "He had a very cheerful nature and whenever the young people planned to go somewhere, he wanted to come along with them. He truly enjoyed life; he always found a good side to every situation."

"He loved to party; he really enjoyed it and he used to spend a lot of time with us. He liked getting together with our group because we were younger than him and besides, he had an enviable strength and, most of all, a great amount of enthusiasm."

According to Mr. Mauricio Rioseco's opinion, "there is one thing I am especially grateful for: when I first met Mr. Kahan ten years ago, he was a man with 50 years of experience in his company, a man who was very successful and knew every trick in the book regarding his line of work. When I was eighteen years old I had already come to many dead ends when dealing with several people. But in him I found a man who had the courtesy of listening to me right from my very first comment. After having listened to my words and having thought about whether what I had said made sense or not, he gave me the opportunity to become one of his close friends and establish a tight relationship with the Kahan family. And that was forever. Some very successful people are very reserved in their treatment towards younger people. That is why I thank him so much: he gave me my self-confidence and encouraged me to take the next step. Wulf's attitude was extremely important for the company. With my father's help he started trusting me; that really meant a lot to me; the things I learned from him are priceless."

Dr. Miguel Ángel Gil adds that "Mr. Wulf Kahan had a marvelous sense of parenthood. He always treated us in a special way, with the deference that any man would have towards his children's friends."

Lourdes Gil continues: "He was a charming person, one of the nicest I've ever met. Due to the fact that my father died when I was very young, I think I would have loved to have a dad like him."

Dr. Carlos Rossell stresses on the interest Wulf Kahan had, being the head of his family, in the academic aspects of his children's lives and in everything that concerned their personal development: "Wulf participated very intensely in Ari's education, and mine. He was interested in knowing which were the courses we were taking at school and several times, while we were all sitting at the table during lunch, he would ask our opinion on the country's situation and about the world view in general. Wulf Kahan did not grieve over his lack of academic education; he was proud of what he had accomplished and didn't even think of what he didn't have. I met him through Ari, who was my friend and classmate at the National School of Economics at the UNAM[26]."

"I remember we were both very courteous with each other and that evolved into a mutual feeling of affection. I always felt a lot of appreciation for Wulf and had great respect for him. He was like a father to me; besides, he was more or less the same age as my mom. As a matter of fact, he treated me as if he were my father."

"Don Wulf's personality was a very rich one: he was a man with an intense joy for living, with an enormous ability to work. Except for the days in which we spent our vacations together, I never saw him in an idle state."

Mr. Alberto Liz affirms that Wulf Kahan was very proud of having started out with almost nothing: "he wasn't a person who suffered from complexes regarding his origins. On the contrary, he wanted everyone to know how it was that he had started his business; the very difficult situations he had to go through. I think his main quality was his honesty: he was a man with an integrity that passed any test."

Regarding this same aspect, Dr. Carlos Rossell speaks again: "He didn't get a college education, nevertheless, he was very much aware of the importance of giving his

[26] *National Autonomous University of Mexico*

children a higher academic education. I believe that the example we got from Wulf, watching how successfully he raised his family and the love he had for his wife, was an education in real life for his four children; he taught them how to build the best foundations in their own families."

However, Mr. Francisco Torrado Haza remembers that Wulf Kahan once told him that "you never know how things will turn out in the end: one of my grandchildren stopped studying after finishing high school because he said that he knew more than what his teachers did; and there you have him, just look at all the things he has accomplished without having gone to university. He is a great businessman now."

"In the school of life you have the place you want to give yourself. I couldn't get a proper academic education, but I believe life itself teaches us many things: it is a daily teaching that we must learn from."

"I wouldn't say that Adolfo was a very religious person," *Luis Kahan continues.* "He was rather more of a believer and a traditionalist. He never missed the services for the major religious holidays. He was a man who was very respected within the Jewish community and was very generous in his contributions. He gave the community some very special presents, including a silver *Hannukiyah*[27] and a *Torah*[28] he gave to the Beth-El Congregation when he celebrated his 50th wedding anniversary."

[27] *Nine arm candelabrum.*
[28] *Jewish Holy Scriptures of The Old Testament.*

Mr. Francisco Plancarte comments: "One of the things we have appreciated more about Wulf and Estelita is their understanding nature, that ecumenical sense they have always had in them. Always respectful. He was very much appreciated within the Jewish community, but he had excellent Christian friends, as well."

"I traveled many times with them and they always made sure that I fulfilled my obligations as a Catholic during those trips," *adds Dr. Carlos Rossell.* "They have attended several Catholic ceremonies and I have also been present during Jewish ones. Both our families have experienced ecumenism. Mr. Wulf and Estela showed great respect for my religion and were interested in knowing its principles. This is probably what has brought us even closer."

"Without a doubt, Wulf was a man with a very strong personality," *says CPA Daniel González D'Bejarle,* "he was a character. What I remember the most about him is that he felt very proud of himself, of his life, of his accomplishments, of his fulfillment. I don't mean that he was proud in the sense of being vain or arrogant; on the contrary, he was aware that he had fought long and hard to reach his goals, not only regarding money, but also where his family and his business were concerned, as well as with everything else in which he was successful."

"Wulf was very cordial," *Mr. Francisco Plancarte continues,* "but he was a man of a very strong nature, as well. I am not saying that he was domineering, he just wasn't the type of person who would hesitate when taking a decision; far from that, he knew exactly what he wanted. All his actions were absolutely honest; always."

Mr. Emilio Sánchez Peláez adds the following words, which further describe Wulf's strength of character:

"Behind every great man, there's a great woman, and there is no better example of this old saying than the case of Wulf and Estela Kahan. Estela modulated Wulf, she appeased him. She was a very intelligent, very humane woman. She was very protective of her children: like all mothers, she wanted to have all her children gathered around her and, since she was extremely smart, she succeeded at that. Wulf showed his insides of steel, his strong character, without becoming a grouch. He always had a smile on his lips and laughed at people's jokes, nevertheless, he did have a very strong character."

This personality of great contrasts is outlined by the most varied comments; Mr. Juan José Ortega affirms that "Wulf Kahan was always extremely nice to everyone. I never saw him in a bad mood and we treated each other in a very pleasant manner. The courtesies the Kahan family had towards my wife are things that I will always be grateful for."

"The love he had for life is still shown through the many home videos they recorded so their grandchildren could watch them someday and thus, also be proud of their grandfather."

Mr. Saul Rosales mentions that "everyone loved Don Adolfo; a lot of people appreciated him. He felt a great joy for living and knew that life could not be wasted on trying to hide one's flaws. He knew that life was beautiful and one had to face it without fear."

"I remember it was very few times, on very rare occasions, that I saw Adolfo in a state of slight depression. I think he did not even know what real depression was because he always tried to find the good side of life," *Luis Kahan relates.* "I believe there is a good and a bad side to all of us, but Adolfo's good side covered 90 per cent of his personality against a bad side of 10 per cent. True, he would explode all of a sudden. He was very firm in his decisions; he believed in certain things and would not give in; he was very persevering. When he set his mind on something, he would accomplish it, no matter how difficult it was."

"He wanted to keep his family united and for that, he once threw a big party in which he accomplished to get all the Kahan's together."

"Wulf had a great virtue: he was a quiet man; he was never interested in obtaining an important position in society. He always tried to keep a low profile, both in the private and in the social aspects of his life," *says Mr. Isaac Grabinsky.* "He held the position of councilor at the Jewish community's sport center. He was always very elegantly dressed, loved a good drink, a good meal, and a good party. No one ever talked badly about him; not that I recall, anyway."

Mr. Carlos Doring continues describing Wulf Kahan's personality as if he were sketching out an image of him with short quick brush strokes: "He was a fellow who was willing to share his experiences, tell anecdotes, and listen to others, as well. His conversations were very entertaining. He was a person who was proud of his Jewish origins and his physical condition; he was a strong guy, he was a very fit fellow. A man who was always on the move and did things with pleasure. I also remember Wulf could position his fingers in the same unique way that the *Cohanim*[29] used to do, which meant that he was a direct descendant of such group within the Jewish religion."

As it has already been said, Wulf was very respectful towards the Jewish traditions and frequently used to attend the services held at the synagogue. This did not limit his social life in any way. He was always 'the life of the party', he was a true promoter of happiness without ever having worried about time.

"He loved going to parties," *says Salomón, Wulf's oldest brother,* "especially the ones that were held in his honor. He was a great man, hospitable like no one I have ever known, and could stay up until very late at night: he was always the last one to leave. He had such a sociable nature...he could make new friends even if he were standing in the middle of a desert; if there was no one near him, he would go looking for someone to spend his time with."

"He would attract people wherever he went," *adds Raquel, Salomón's wife,* "and my sister-in-law, Estela,

---

[29] *Jewish priests in the times of the Holy Temple in Jerusalem.*

would always play along. They had guests at their place all the time. Adolfo was a very handsome man and also pretty flirty; impeccable all his life; always very well dressed, very elegant. Even when he had already fallen ill and had to sit in his wheel chair, he liked wearing the nicest outfits."

"He was very careful about the way he dressed, whether he was wearing a fancy suit or just casual attire during his vacation trips. Someone once said that Wulf Kahan appreciated all that is beautiful, everything from a sunset to the slender figure of a lovely young woman. He always liked pretty women and whenever he spoke to them, he did it with all politeness and refinement."

Mr. Norberto Cortés remembers that when Wulf Kahan arrived at AMDA, he could see him walking down the corridor "with his inseparable pipe which gave off a very delicate aroma of fine tobacco. It's just as if I could see him now...Don Wulf...always with his pipe and a smile on his face, always so elegant. He was the most decent person I have known in all my life."

Javier Escobar, Wulf Kahan's barber, says that he behaved "with that special charm of his, that attraction...I was amazed by the energy he irradiated. He used to come here to get his hair cut; he liked to look good. He had somewhat of a round face and was a man of strong complexion. He was not very talkative but he would sometimes tell me about his business. He was a man with a lot of future because he would come up with good ideas and would carry them out most of the time."

Mr. Alberto Liz describes Wulf Kahan as "a man who always gave good advice to his fellow men; he was always a positive, loving, hard working, dedicated man. Everyone liked him; there were no ifs or buts about him, no bad memories, no bad comments; not one."

"What I remember about Wulf is his constant personal serenity. He always appeared to be very much in control and sure about his destiny. I clearly remember the look in his eyes: very pleasant, very peaceful; it was the look of a real man."

In the following paragraphs, writer Eduardo Luis Feher stresses on the importance of 'Wulf Kahan's look':

"Every human being has a distinctive quality of his own. In Mr. Wulf Kahan's particular case what probably attracted my attention the most about his whole personality was his eyes."

"It would be too ordinary if I were to say that 'the eyes are the reflection of a person's soul'; nevertheless, I must add that rather just his eyes, the expression in his look is what caught my eye. And that is what I would like to talk about very briefly, as homage to the memory of this man called Wulf Kahan."

"In this world there are as many looks as there are eyes. Although we see the eyes of other people, very few are the times that we are aware of their expression, their look. It is very true that glancing around is not at all the same as looking. In Mr. Kahan's particular case his look reflected many things about him. For one thing, he had a look that was firm, steady...maybe even affably inquisitive."

"His eyes were of a light hue and his verbal expression, in agreement with them."

"Looking at a person like that meant approaching a strong yet open, honest, and direct personality. It was not necessary to hear his voice; with just one simple look from him, you knew -clearly- what mood he was in."

"Mr. Kahan's look could be a sort of biography: perhaps he had seen it all; perhaps he had felt it all; perhaps he had suffered it all...;perhaps -why not?- he had enjoyed it all. Any way, he had a life rich with experiences, with ups and downs, with success, with the warmth of a family, with devotion to his work."

"Give a tribute to Wulf Kahan? Yes, and there are many reasons for it. But maybe the most important is because he knew how to make his family the core of all his desires...and how to raise his children in the best way possible, bequeathing them an example of honesty and hard work, always under the shelter of the millenary, the eternal cloak of Judaism."

"That is why talking about Wulf Kahan's look makes me reflect on those words that the wind will never take away, written years ago by the Chinese-American philosopher Lin-Yutang:

Life...is really a dream, and human beings are like travelers that float along the eternal river of time, embarking at one point and disembarking at another so as to make way for others that are waiting downstream for their turn to come on board. Half of the poetry in life would vanish if we did not believe that it is all a dream, or a trip with people in passing, or simply a stage in which the actors rarely realize that they are only performing a part in a play."

Some of the previous comments have stated that Wulf Kahan loved life in all its expressions, in all its manifestations. He was a man who respected and took good care of his body, being this the reason why he considered exercising as such an important part of his life. As the athletic man he was, he always made sure that his body was in good shape: swimming, diving, weight training, golf...they all formed a part of his everyday life.

"Wulf Kahan played soccer since he was a young man," *says Dr. Fernando Katz,* "and sometime later, fifty years ago, we met when the creation of the *Centro Deportivo Israelita* began. I was the sports center's first president and Adolfo had a very active participation in the creation and the maintenance of the center."

Later, at the Bellavista Golf Club, he started playing golf with Carlos Shapiro, Jose Belkin, and Dr. Katz himself, on Wednesdays and Saturdays; Javier, an employee at the club, says that:

"When he came to play golf, I remember Don Adolfo walking in a sort of slow manner, with his pipe, and he wore a gold chain with an anchor around his neck. He always said hello to everyone and left a delicious scent of tobacco as he passed by. He moved very slowly, very calmly, when he was at the club. He crouched down a little bit as he walked. He greeted everybody. He used to carry some kind of small knife that he would use to loosen the tobacco in his pipe and then he would add some more tobacco to it, since he smoked it all day long. I believe he would only put his pipe down at night while he slept."

"Don Adolfo was truly a good person. I never heard him yell or swear at someone. He wore a chain with a gold charm of an anchor, which looked very nice resting upon his chest. I saw him wearing his sailor hat once or twice; a captain from the Navy would not look as good as he did in that hat. Later, when he fell ill, they would take him to the club for lunch: he would smoke a cigarette -as customary- and drink his whisky. Ever since he became ill, he started smoking Marlboro Light's, not his pipe, not anymore."

Undoubtedly, most of Wulf Kahan's life revolved around cars. As a business, as a hobby, he really enjoyed watching a car's design and, most of all, he enjoyed driving them at full speed.

Don Vicente Ariztegui recalls that "he loved driving. When he went to Miami he would rent a car; in Las Vegas, the very first thing he did upon his arrival was rent a car, and it had to be a new model, too. He used to drive at very high speeds...the windows down (back then the cars didn't have an air conditioning system as they do nowadays), and a cigarette in his hand, at speeds of 95 to 110 miles per hour. And I would tell him:

'Hey pal, hold your horses! Speed down a little!'

Wulf's nephew, Samuel Kahan, comments:

"He liked doing everything at the speed of light: he drove at high speeds and that scared me. Whenever we traveled to Acapulco I would tell him that he could drive his car there and I would travel by plane because he loved to experience thrills that were just too much for me to handle. I believe it would take him three hours and a half to get to Acapulco; he was mad! He was very lucky, he was a good driver, but the truth is that at those speeds... Luck was always on his side. And the same thing happened when we were on board the yacht: we went so fast we would fly!"

"Adolfo used to tell me that he liked sailing because when he was a kid he used to cross the Nieper River back in Russia," *Estela Kahan remembers.* "As soon as he could, he bought himself a motor boat and we were always related with the sea in some way. When we went to our first beach house in Acapulco for the first time, he felt so happy that he wanted to invite everyone over and he went to the beach to invite the people there to come in: and he didn't even know them!"

'Make us some hot soup,' he would tell me. How could he think of having hot soup in Acapulco? But it was fine with me, I loved seeing him so happy. I used to feel seasick when we went out on the yacht, but thanks to him I learned how to be a full-fledged sailor and not feel nauseous. I would always come along with him when he traveled; there were very few times when he made a trip without me."

Mr. Samy Cohen says that "Wulf Kahan had a yacht and he invited me once to come along for a sail with his wife and some other friends. He served a delicious meal that his wife had prepared. I was very impressed when Wulf, who was as strong as any twenty-year-old, dove into the sea to go for a swim. I remember this very fondly because our relationship was one of mutual understanding. We were constantly eager to talk about many things, including anything regarding today's social, political, and moral issues. For me, those conversations form a part of very dear moments I shared with Wulf."

"He had bought an apartment on William Island in Miami and he then showed me his true and sincere friendship through a very thoughtful act on his part: he had seen an apartment just like his, he told me about it, and I gave him the money to buy it. I did it just because I knew that that way I was going to have him and his wife as our neighbors."

Dr. Miguel Jusidman says: "Among all the things that remain fresh in my mind about Adolfo is the image of a strong man who always had a very clear idea of what he wanted, a man who was always aware of what happened around him, always very alert."

"Whenever he was on board his yacht he was just like a little child playing with his favorite toy. He knew he was an excellent host; you could see that he was proud of all that he did. He was very courteous; a man who took care of his guests, and asked questions, and was very considerate about the people he was with."

"Every time I was near him I felt that our relationship was a very affectionate one, yet he was not overly sentimental. He would come to me and show his affection in his own particular way, without being corny. He was not a softy, never. I felt very comfortable when I was close to him."

One of Wulf Kahan's greatest loves was the sea. There was constantly some kind of connection between it and Wulf's life. And as Mr. Oscar Siegal says: "the man had an apartment in Acapulco: it was his palace. He invited us over to his place a few times. Perla, his daughter, also invited us and some other friends to their apartment and Adolfo would approach me and say:

'Come on, leave those kids alone and let's go play some golf.'

"Judging by his age, he could have been my father-in-law because he was twenty years older than me, yet he always treated me as his friend. I have very fond memories about Adolfo. My wife called him 'uncle Fito'. Wulf was a very tough and strict man, but mostly a very honest man, as well. As a matter of fact, he was a splendid and very generous host. I never did anything for Wulf to be so nice to me. I also recall he never got tired when he was in Acapulco."

He was enchanted by that port and the comment made by Mr. Alberto López de Nava talks, precisely, about the city of Acapulco:

"My father-in-law wanted to buy an apartment there and one day he met a man called Wulf Kahan who told him he was selling his. During their conversation the automobile topic came up and they also talked about Wulf's grandchildren, who also worked in the car business. My father-in-law told him that he was looking for another apartment for his children, besides the one he already had."

"Since my father-in-law had the habit of making verbal deals, they agreed on a price for the apartment and all the furnishings. My father-in-law gave Wulf an advance payment and, supposedly, he was going to go to Acapulco later on, but he couldn't."

"The day came when the rest of the payment was due and my father-in-law called me and told me he was worried because they hadn't talked about what was in the apartment and he was afraid that something might have been changed, that they had taken some things from the apartment or that it might be totally empty. 'I know that family,' I told him, 'and I assure you nothing will be missing.' And so he completed the payment."

"When he went back to Acapulco, my father-in-law was surprised when he realized that there was, in fact, something missing in the apartment: the dust; that was gone for sure because they had even cleaned the place spotless."

Mr. Agustín Velasco says: "In Acapulco we found that we were both staying at the same place because my father had bought a place in the same building in which Wulf Kahan had his apartment: the Acapulco Tower. He had dedicated a lot of time and love to that place throughout the years. He sold the apartment to my father and sometimes we met there during vacations."

"Wulf was a very kind and affectionate person and was very healthy, too. He exercised often and was always concerned about staying fit. He loved the sea and when he was away from his business life, he liked spending his time with his children and grandchildren. He was a fine sailor and had plans for a trip to the Gulf of California, in which he was going to call at several ports where some of his relatives would get off and some others would come on board."

"There are people who have very busy lives and don't include their family in their plans. Not him. He looked very good in a bathing suit. I remember he had a very cheerful personality and enjoyed life to the most. He was a very simple person, as well."

Samuel Kahan remembers that Wulf "was in a swimsuit one time we went to Acapulco and my wife commented that his body was not that of a man his age. He was really strong, very firmly built muscles, and had the appearance of a young man; it was amazing. Further more, I can't say that he was too much of an athlete, which made it even more admirable. One thing that really 'bugged' me was that when we stayed there, in his apartment, we would go out at night, went partying and then came back home at dawn, and yet, he would wake us up at seven o'clock in the morning. He enjoyed being awake and slept very few hours; even we, the younger members of the family, could not keep up with him. He wouldn't rest, not for a minute. I can't remember him ever being a passive person; he was always on the go."

Arie Derzavich comments:

"The first experience I remember sharing with my grandfather was in Acapulco. Every time we went there he wanted to have all his family together, all the time, from the first moment when he woke us up in the early hours of the morning so we could all have breakfast at the same time. Then we would go to the yacht and he would appoint each person with a chore; every single one of us was responsible for doing something before going to the yacht: the house chores, buying the food for lunch, and all those kinds of things. When it came to food, Spanish sausages and crisp pork rind were the two dishes he liked best and he would prepare them on board. He was the captain, all the time; that's the image I have of him in my mind, not only as the captain on board the yacht, but also as the head of the family. You could say he was our captain."

"Every time before turning the ignition on he would adopt a very serious attitude and, in a very formal manner, he would tell us about the precautions we had to keep in mind while on board. There was no joking around at that time, everything was of great importance. Then we would sail off to a certain place. We often went to Pichilingue beach and once there, he turned into just another one of the kids. He knew exactly how to act accordingly with each moment."

"And in the afternoon, as part of a discipline and because the Yacht Club closed at that time, we would head back home always at six. Then, he would once again go back to being the serious and formal captain so he could carefully bring the yacht back in the docks. There were no more jokes and he would not let me steer the yacht in. Very rare times he let my uncles Ari and Jack do it, but not always because he was the one responsible for all of us and the one in charge."

Hace 50 Años, el 21 de Junio de 1936

Estela y Wulf Kahan

Fueron unidos en matrimonio.
Sus hijos, nietos y bisnietos no fuimos
invitados a esta ceremonia.
Para reparar esta perdonable omisión,
están de acuerdo en reconformar su matrimonio,
exactamente 50 años después.

Será para nosotros un gran honor contar
con su presencia como testigos de la renovación
de sus votos matrimoniales; en la Ceremonia
y Cocktail que ofreceremos el sábado 21
de Junio de 1986 a las 18:00 Hrs. en punto,
en la Congregación Bet - El de México.
Horacio 1722 Col. Polanco.

Hijos:

Avi, Betty, Pedro, Fish,
Ruthy, Pepe, Jack, Tuta.

Nietos:

Saúl, Irene, Patty, Bernardo,
Carlos, Ana, Heidy, Jorge, Jackie, Avie,
Sammy, Jaime, Sandra, Sandra, Gabriela,
Daniel, Gabriel, Italiana.

Bisnietos:

Beppy y Tali

Invitation to Wulf and Estela Kahan's 50th wedding anniversary celebration, organized by their children, grandchildren, and great-grandchildren.

Wulf Kahan's last appearance at AMDA. Monterrey Convention, 1992; accompanied by Jorge

CHAPTER VIII

The Road to
Freedom

Freedom, Sancho, is one of the most precious gifts that Heaven has bestowed upon men; no treasures that earth holds buried or the sea conceals can compare with it; for freedom, as for honor, life may and should be ventured; and on the other hand, captivity is the greatest evil that can fall to the lot of man.[30]

The History of Don Quixote de la Mancha
Miguel de Cervantes Saavedra

[30] *Translated by John Ormsby for Encyclopaedia Britannica, Inc., Great Books of the Western World, Vol. 29, pg. 379, William Benton Publisher, 19th printing, USA, 1971.*

Wulf Kahan's road to freedom, in which he had the time to prepare his encounter with God, lasted more than two years; it was a period full of the most contrary and diverse emotions. A man who was strong, active, full of life, all of a sudden, found himself confined to a wheel chair. In 1990, the goals Wulf Kahan had set for himself were completely changed by a surgical accident. Not everything was over for him; now, the road that his life was to follow would be different; difficult and filled with obstacles, of course, but with patience, with faith, with perseverance, he would be able to do well, as he most certainly did. Some of the people who spent some time with Wulf during his period of illness have collaborated in many ways in order to create this chapter. Such is the case of Phil Steinberg, the therapist who treated Wulf in Miami and now narrates his encounter with him:

"When I saw him for the first time, it seemed to me that Wulf was somewhere near his 70's; he was sitting in a wheel chair, nevertheless, I was able to realize that he was a strong man, of a muscular physique, and was probably about 5 feet 6 inches high. He must have been a marvelous man in his youth; he had blue eyes and gray hair, perfectly combed."

"He was impeccably dressed in a new pair of tennis shoes and a modern jogging suit. Around him, just in case he needed anything, were his wife, his oldest son, a chauffeur, a nurse, and another two members of his family."

"The whole group approached me; he came forward in his wheel chair and extended his left hand to me and said:

'I'm Wulf Kahan.'

"This was the beginning of the road that I walked along the side of Adolfo Wulf Kahan. From that moment on life would never be the same again for either one of us."

"Wulf called his chauffeur and spoke to him in fast and clear Spanish. The chauffeur then translated his words:

'I came to Miami to see a doctor, to see if he could help me overcome this but I do not feel satisfied and have abandoned my therapy treatment. One day I was at a shopping mall trying to get into my car and a person who had been watching me for a while came up to me and told me that if I wanted to come out of this state there was only one person who could help me: Phil and only Phil; he's the reason I'm still here, he said to me.' Wulf looked me straight in the eyes and again he said 'Here I am.' He was never able to tell me who was that other mystery person who had recommended me to him."

"I immediately called the physician who had been taking care of him so as to find out more about what conditions he was in. I got the information I needed and at that time I started talking to Wulf with his chauffeur's help who told me:

'My boss says that we must have faith,' and Wulf and I stared into each other's eyes. A few seconds later a smile lit up Wulf's face and he repeated: 'Yes...faith.'

"When Wulf and I looked into each other's eyes I realized that in that look of his, so strong, I could find all the answers to the questions I had regarding him. It was obvious that I could count on his full cooperation and faith."

"After this, his wife, Estela, and Ari, his oldest son, introduced themselves to me and asked me what kind of therapeutic program I had in mind for Wulf. They also offered me their help and provided me with the medical history of his illness. We then said good-bye and made plans for an appointment the next day. When they had already left several people that worked at the rehabilitation center approached me and asked who was 'that very interesting man' who seemed to be very wealthy."

"I will not go into details concerning the description of his illness or the damages it caused him. I will only talk about the man and not his surgical accident; I will only say that Wulf suffered a massive stroke that left him partially paralyzed from head to toes."

"The next day we started working on a very ambitious program: we had to increase his quality of life by intensifying the things that he was still able to do. Could we get him to walk again? The answer to this was always: with God's help we would fight to death to make this happen."

"Back then there were three young men working with me and Wulf loved joking around with all of them, but especially with Sam: they would arm wrestle each other, and fight each other, and insult one another as if they were little children. The girls at the gymnasium used to flirt with him and everyone watched him work hard, amazed by his effort."

"As time went by, Wulf gained more strength and was able to walk a few steps with the aid of his walking stick. At that time, walking even a little rised his spirits and he would do demonstrations for other stroke patients, showing them the things that were possible for them to accomplish."

"We had numerous breakthroughs as well as set backs; sometimes the effort was so enormous that Wulf would get angry and shouted: enough, enough enough!"

"The entire Kahan family, children and sons and daughters-in-law, were always there to support him, encourage him and inspire him not to give up despite the uncertainty that the future held regarding a successful outcome."

"With great satisfaction I came to realize that, in fact, Wulf was a very, very wealthy man, not so much because of his material possessions, but rather for his affections. After eight months had gone by, he had gained control over his face, his arms, his torso, and overall, he had had a pretty good recovery. His control over his respiratory process was excellent, and he was starting to show signs of movement in parts of his body where there had been prior paralysis."

"We were all very excited about these improvements, but very tired, as well. Wulf asked me to design a rehabilitation program for him and wanted me to come back to Mexico with him."

"As soon as I arrived in Mexico City I was taken in by the Kahan family, I really was. We had become truly good and sincere friends, Estela, Ari, and I...'daddy, daddy'...these were the words that were mentioned thousands of times during the period I spent with him."

" Sam accompanied me to Mexico and the prank war between Wulf and him was one of the decisive factors in the rehabilitation process. On one occasion Wulf asked Sam to taste a very hot *salsa* and he felt he nearly died because of how hot it was: his face changed colors to a bright red. Those were happy days for us; we were reaching our goal. Wulf's quality of life was improving and if there was not going to be a full recovery, at least there had been a major breakthrough: we had learned to live with Wulf's illness, both him and us."

"I returned home to Miami knowing that Wulf would not give up. One month later, Ari called to tell me that Wulf would be visiting me again in Miami for part of what had been achieved through my work with him had been lost and he knew we could recover it all in Miami."

"I wish that in case something like that ever happened to me my children would do for me the same as Ari did for his father. Here we all feel a profound affection towards him. Any father would give it all to receive such dedication and love from his child. May God bless you, Ari."

"Ari once commented that, being AMDA's president. he would have to attend a very important event: the Association's convention. He felt very proud about having achieved such an important goal and told me that it would be necessary to prepare Wulf for his attendance to the event that would take place in the city of Monterrey. So I hung a huge banner at the entrance to the gymnasium that read *'The Road To Monterrey'* and every time that Wulf arrived at the gym he would see it and read it."

"The two of us set the goals that would lead us to Monterrey; he told me he did not want to make a big deal out of it and that, besides all, that was Ari's moment, not his."

"We had to act with courage and, most of all, with perseverance, precisely the way Wulf did during the four months we had to prepare him. I gave him a strong, balanced, and agile training program, as well as respiratory development exercises to fight the psychological trauma. That was our goal and that was our golden opportunity."

"Ari and Jack constantly came up with new ideas for their father's recovery: driving golf carts, visiting boat expositions, learning to use a computer, sailing...things that were easy to do and ingenious; anything that could motivate Wulf. One time his son Jack took some videos of him in the gymnasium which clearly show his effort and courage."

"Those four months went by very quickly; my wife and I traveled to Monterrey with Wulf and Estela and there we found ourselves facing an event that surpassed all our expectations."

"Hundreds of people were gathered in the auditorium on the first day of the convention: the press and the television media were there and they were expecting the President of Mexico to attend the event, as well as various representatives from Canada and the United States. The event had been given the name of *The Encounter of the Americas*."

"As the plane ride had been very long and tedious, Wulf was feeling tired; besides, upon his arrival he had attended several conferences and meetings, as well as celebrations and social reunions in which many of his old friends were present."

"Wulf was having a good time, however, he seemed to be in an introspective mood; I began to have my doubts about whether I had prepared him well enough for an effort of such magnitude."

"The main part of the event was going to take place the day after that. In an enormous room, filled with the presence of a splendid audience, Ari took the stage as the main speaker and addressed the public in the auditorium. All the Kahan family was there to offer him their support."

"Wulf was sitting in a seat of honor: in the first row, right in the center. He seemed to be very pensive; he was living a great experience with his friends, his family, as if that single event represented the conjunction of all his moments of success."

"Ari delivered a marvelous speech and received a generous round of applause from his audience. After the representative of the President of Mexico, Mr. Andrés Caso Lombardo, had taken the floor, something happened that surprised us all: during Mr. Caso's speech I turned to look to where Wulf was sitting and he asked me to approach him. Something was happening and Wulf whispered to my ear: 'The Road to Monterrey...' For a moment I remained motionless and reacted only when he asked me to pull his wheel chair back about 100 feet and then he told me: 'Stop.' At that moment I realized that Wulf was going to go for the acid test and then I saw that we were about 150 feet away from the podium."

"He straightened his posture, stood up, grabbed his walking stick, and started to walk. The people pulled their eyes away from the podium and turned to look at Wulf standing on his own two feet; and they applauded non-stop until he had completed his walk up the 150-foot corridor. It was an intense round of applause; it was incredible."

"Wulf was a man who had always loved life and right there and then he showed everyone that he had faced a challenge, despite that he was already exhausted by then. I saw tears roll down Ari's cheeks; family and friends, they were all caught in the emotion of the moment."

"This is one of the times in which the word 'man' is defined in the clearest way possible: when a man's actions surpass the expectations of all those around him."

"May God be with you, Wulf Kahan. Shalom."

In spite of his illness, Wulf was still an active person with the obvious restrictions of a man who finds himself stuck to a wheel chair. Nevertheless, he continued going to his office at Kahan Automotriz *and attending the meetings held by the AMDA Board of Directors and other organizations. As a matter of fact, in May of 1992, he still participated in the 38th Dealers Convention.*

Mr. Agustín Arriaga Rivera says, "I had the pleasure of the greeting Wulf, my admired and friend, and giving him a big hug on Monday, May 25th, at our Chrysler reunion."

Mr. Werner Gunnar also comments: "I met Mr. Kahan when I started working for Chrysler, which was then called *Fábrica Automex*. He was a man with integrity and a fine example for all, a man you could always learn something from. I had the opportunity to see him this past Monday, May 25th during the inauguration of the 38th Chrysler Dealers Convention."

Wulf Kahan wished to participate in the most number of activities as was possible. Already in a wheel chair, he received an invitation from Don Arturo Pérez to attend the inauguration of the Automobile Museum. The host made his way through a large crowd in order to personally greet Wulf, who was very excited to be there. During Don Arturo's and Wulf's tour through the museum they took the time to admire each car individually, and as they mentioned each one of the makes and models they were both so moved that they found it almost impossible to hold back the tears. In their conversation one could notice the pride they felt about having lived through a great period of the Mexican automotive industry, which would be remembered from that day forth thanks to the creation of this museum.

Some people comment about the impression Wulf made in his efforts not to let himself give up, not to crumble, despite his illness.

"I met him once he had already fallen ill," *says therapist Guillo Maldonado, the trainer that helped him in Mexico City.* "We developed a type of friendship that is not easily found, for it is very difficult to grow a 'cold-climate fruit in hot-climate regions.' We both belonged to very different societies, nevertheless, I found a true human being in Mr. Kahan."

"In spite of our differences in status I found it very easy to make him my friend. He was interested in my life: he knew I liked writing and he would often ask me about that; I read several of my poems to him and I also recorded some songs for him."

"Mr. Wulf was a very charitable person, however, he did not want anyone to know it. I once saw how he donated a wheel chair to a man whose last name was Albino and who worked as a public accountant for the Department of Treasury and had been paralyzed for more than sixteen years. Since Mr. Wulf did not want others to know that he helped people out, he arranged everything almost secretly; this only proved the importance of a man who planned everything he did with great care. This time it had been premeditated; no treachery or taking advantage of anyone or anything: he bought an electric wheel chair, a beautiful one, which he himself gave the man."

"Carlos was the owner of the Nautilios gymnasium located on kilometer 15 of the Mexico-Toluca highway. When Mr. Wulf arrived at the gym he would just stand there until Carlos raised his head to realize that he was there and greeted him. That's the way he acted with everybody; he would never brag about his wealth: he was an ocean that never thought of the lakes as being inferior and, even more so, never criticized a pond."

"He was a man with a strong, tough, imposing appearance but deep inside he was tender and so sincere that I would say his strength was only the mask behind which he used to hide himself."

Mr. Fernando Castro, who for many years worked with Wulf Kahan, says that after he fell ill "he would come over in his wheel chair and he once gave it to me in order to repair it because it was an electric wheel chair. I spent quite some time working on it and even I put rearview mirrors on the arms and a horn like the ones used in antique cars, the ones with a round rubber air pump on one end. That made him laugh a lot and from time to time he would still joke around, but not as much as he did before he fell ill."

"He also thought it was pretty funny when I put the bicycle rearview mirrors on his wheel chair: the only mirrors I could find were enameled in bright blue, but there was nothing I could do about it...there were no others available."

Mr. Fernando Cohen relates that Wulf Kahan "asked me to have an elevator installed at the *Nissan Interlomas* dealership and I told him that I would not do it because he was still perfectly capable of walking up the stairs and, in fact, he was. When I realized, as time went by, that he was starting to get tired very easily, I had no choice but to have the elevator installed. He came to visit me one afternoon (I believe it was one or two weeks before he passed away) and the installation of the elevator had been completed just the day before. He used it for the very first time that same day."

Even during the time when he was ill, Wulf Kahan continued encouraging and offering his advice to the young people that knew him for one reason or another. Regarding this, Mr. Pablo Guerra says: "I remember that one of the things that impressed me the most about Mr. Kahan was the strength he showed during his period of illness. I met him a long time ago and always respected and admired him. I was amazed, most of all, the times when he stood up from his wheel chair; he was able to do it, so he would stand on his feet and stay that way throughout the National Anthem whenever he attended a ceremony. Thus, he proved that letting yourself fall was not the way to face things; he knew that, no matter what happened, one must always keep on going."

"I also recall that when he went to watch the car races at the racetrack *Magdalena Mixuca*, in spite of the difficulties it represented for him to get there, we would help him up the bleachers and I can still see his face light up with joy when he heard the engines roar."

Mr. Hernán Figueroa Cal y Mayor narrates that he "received an invitation from Mr. Ari Kahan to attend the AMDA Assembly that would be held in Monterrey. I knew that two important occurrences would be taking place during the event: the first was the culmination of the work of an enterprising person and the end of a dignified and honorable administration; and the second was that I knew that Wulf, Ari's father, was going to face a challenge they had called 'The Road to Monterrey'. As a matter of fact, during the ceremony I witnessed how Mr. Kahan stood up, pushing his wheel chair aside, and started walking with his head up high, looking at his son. The silence spread all over the auditorium and it was an amazing thing to see. We were all moved by the sight of that man walking down the corridor, slowly, but with great dignity."

"When the ceremony had ended, I approached Mr. Kahan and asked him if I could give him a hug. I felt that he was moved by this for just a few moments and I knew that I was hugging the man who had gathered enough courage and enough strength so as to overcome his own illness."

Through her comments, Dr. Irma Carrillo, a specialist in physical therapy, reinforces the concepts expressed in the previous paragraphs:

"When times are too difficult to bear, when the circumstances are unfavorable, that is when an exceptional human being proves his worth. It's easy to be magnanimous when things are going well; it's easy to be blessed when the circumstances are favorable; but only the person who has showed his or her courage and has been magnanimous during tough times is the one who is worthy of the honors that life has in store for him or her. Adolfo Kahan was one of those people."

Dr. José Cheirif, grandson-in-law to Wulf Kahan, has sent the following text from New Orleans:

"Three incidents in grandfather Kahan's life, in which I was involved, render a very good idea of what a special person he was:"

"The first incident happened approximately four years ago. Grandfather Wulf had decided to buy a new boat and knowing that Heidy and I were coming over to Miami to see it, he waited for us to get there and then bought it that weekend. He asked me to go with him to take a look at the boats he had selected; he spent hours showing me the features and disadvantages of each boat so I would have the necessary information so as to help him decide which one to buy. Although it was very likely that he had already made his choice, he wanted to let me know that I was important to him, even if he was aware that I did not know the first thing about boats. He just did it to make me feel good."

"The second incident took place during his visit to Houston some two and a half years ago. He came to Houston to get a check-up because he had been suffering severe chest pains. The heart catheterism the doctors performed on him showed that his main artery was seriously occluded and so were three other coronary arteries."

"The doctors' opinion was unanimous: they recommended that Wulf undergo a coronary bypass surgery. All of a sudden, grandfather Wulf found himself in a very difficult situation; he had to decide whether to have the operation or not; either prevent the risk of sudden death or heart failure in the future or take those risks and live a very restricted life. Fearful of what the outcome of the operation would be, he finally accepted to take the risk and have the surgery. Unfortunately, although the operation did help his heart, there were some complications and he suffered a stroke, which killed the main reason why he had decided to undergo surgery in the first place: to have the opportunity of leading a full and active life."

"Finally, I witnessed the third incident after he had just suffered the stroke: he had been deprived of certain abilities to perform his regular daily activities, which caused him to sink into a state of depression that he would never be able to overcome. Even if he felt very upset with me and the doctors who had treated him, he was never disrespectful towards me and tried to make me feel a part of his family until the last moment."

"These three things show that grandfather Kahan was a person with the power to make others feel good and important when they were around him. He was the kind of person who believed that living life to the maximum was of most importance and, finally, a man who considered his family to be a primordial part of his existence."

Mr. Roberto Zapata Gil has written the following memory about Wulf Kahan:

"During all the years that I have been involved in the hotel industry, and considering that being in charge of managing a hotel one has more contact with the clients than being the captain of a boat, I have met and dealt in a very personal way with many people, everything from great personalities -such as our nation's and other countries' presidents, princes, world famous artists, painters, violinists, singers, and great entrepreneurs- to even the most dishonest and amoral people."

"Of this colorful mosaic of personalities, I especially and affectionately remember my friend Wulf Kahan, who I met around 1958 and who I had a very close relationship with. He was a friend of my father's because of the car dealing business, but he was also his competitor."

"The company I worked for gave me, when I was only 26 years of age, the opportunity to open and run what was then the most luxurious hotel in Acapulco. In those times Acapulco was not a port with the international prestige it has nowadays: it was almost unthinkable for a hotel to have wall to wall carpeting, air conditioning systems, maitre D's, vintage wine cellars, etc., and this made it difficult for the business to get off to a good start."

"Wulf, who was already a very successful man, sensed this from the first moment and, maybe, when he realized how worried I was about it, he wanted me to feel that I was not the only one. Probably due to the fact that he was aware of how important it was for Mexico to have tourism and hotels of such category, he became my most dynamic promoter without ever asking for special treatment or any other thing in return. It was thanks to him that important companies, such as Chrysler, always considered us as an element to help promote motivation among their staff and distributors; thanks to him, they organized their meetings and conventions in Acapulco."

"This meant that we would spend a lot of time together, him and me, in order to create the convention programs and even solve any transportation problems, since the aspect of traveling to Acapulco was very deficient back then."

"Wulf was a man who always liked the sea and he even had several very elegant captain outfits. This was the reason why many of their meetings were held in Acapulco. When he coordinated everything at the events, he would dre s up in his captain suits, kepi, stripes, and all. The best t ing about Wulf is that he didn't only do it once: year a ter year it was him who organized these events. He was a p rson that won the affection and gratitude of those who knew him: he was friends with all our staff, all the people of A apulco; everyone from the boatmen, to the cab drivers, to the bankers, to the local authorities. He was a man with good connections and enjoyed life to its fullest without neglecting his responsibility to form a first class family and a group of very successful companies. And, although Wulf cannot go sailing at the present time, he can surely look back and feel great satisfaction and pride for what he accomplished. I have no doubt whatsoever that many people will remember him dearly, and so will I."

Mr. Jim Hedges, who sailed with Wulf Kahan in many occasions, sends these words from Miami:

"My wife Dimitri and I met Wulf Kahan and his wife in 1988, back when he was planning on buying a yacht. Having proved several times that our friendship was a solid one and having lost my grandparents at a very young age, I always considered Wulf to be the grandfather I never had. I loved hearing him talk about his upbringing since he left Europe to his arrival in America and about the things his family had accomplished."

"I was extremely shocked when he became paralyzed after his surgical accident but this did not diminish the affection, the friendship, the communication we had always had between us. During the period of his illness, I considered it more important than before to take good care of him, therefore, I decided to take him out sailing with me several times. On some occasions I received the help of my uncle Jim, who later worked for Wulf and Doña Estela, acting as chauffeur, cook, housekeeper, nurse, and whatever was necessary; he even assisted in helping him get into the swimming pool."

"I felt excited to see how Wulf fought to overcome that terrible illness and managed to walk with the aid of his walking stick and talk with us. On one occasion, I took the liberty of taking him to see some boats and I remember that, in spite of everything, he was still planning trips which, unfortunately, he was not able to make."

"The last time I saw him, when he came to Miami - because his wish was to return home to be with his people- he told me: 'I've lived a full life, now I am ready to die in peace and I want to die in Mexico.' In my eyes, Wulf was always a true fighter that never gave up. I will forever miss and fondly remember all the moments we spent together, from the time I first met him until the very end."

Mr. Jaime Edid Laham remembers the difficult times that the Kahan family went through:

"My dearest Wulf...he received us at his hospital suite with a sad look on his face, without his usual spark, without his big spontaneous smile...he was too sad and too angry. Estela, my extraordinary Estela, accompanied by Perla, Ari, Ruth, and Jack, commented that during the open heart surgery there had been an 'accident' and due to it my dear friend Wulf would not be self-sufficient for some time. This 'vehicle' he used from then on because of his physical state was the only one out of al the vehicles he ever owned that I did not like one bit."

Mr. Saul Delgado remembers that in the last phase of Wulf Kahan's life "he called me at home one Saturday at about 9:30 in the morning: he had just found out through the news on TV that the Soviet Communist party had seized to exist. He was quite restless and told me that he would be in his office some time later in the morning. Since he was already sick and it was Saturday I really didn't think that he was going to go to work that day; however, I had already arrived at the office when they let me know that 'Don Adolfo is coming up the stairs just now,' so I went o greet him. He kept on walking through the office bu lding and down the corridor until he reached the board ro m because he had to talk to his father Szewel, in the photo that had been placed in that room, and so he did. He invited me to stay there with him. And he talked about the fact that he had witnessed the birth of the Communist party and of the USSR, and about that having been the reason why they had had to leave their homeland; and now, he was witnessing their death. After this, the memories started coming back and he told me about many things regarding his origins, his trip to America his arrival in Cuba where he couldn't leave the ship..."

Professor Alberto Lozano de la Vega says:

"Wulf Kahan: a great man is he who times of difficulty knows how to be generous with others."

"Wulf Kahan did not live his life in vain. He was a man who knew how to cherish the golden nobleness and honesty of a man in a way that only a person who has led a full life can, not problem-free, but surely free of bitterness; a person that when put to the test in the peak of his life, like a new-born child, he again started searching and learning the way of doing things from the very beginning."

"When faced with tough experiences that would destroy any other person's life, he learned to read the bright story of he who has the ability of writing straight on the crooked lines of life without paying attention to superficial appearances. His story was rich in good outcomes."

"The most reliable aspect of his life was also his most important enterprise: his beautiful family, which clearly had his same vision and now takes the baton, passed on by him, to keep it going."

"New energy, which without any doubt will enrich, with its own point of view, the actions of the great old man they learned to love so."

Cantor, Mr. Leibele Jinich has sent us the following text:

"On one occasion, Zev Ben Shaul-Hakohen,[31] Wulf Z"L and Estela came to my office expressing their desire to donate a thirteen arm Menorah for its use in the BNEY and BNOT-MITZVAH[32] celebrations."

"Some time later, Wulf Z"L himself came to our synagogue's facilities one day and let me know that he wanted to donate a Sefer Torah, the sacred parchment scrolls containing the Five Holy Books of Moses, to our congregation. Both, the Menorah and the Torah, now embellish the religious services held at Beth-El. At each Bar or Bat-mitzvah the candelabra glows with its presence and the Holy Scrolls are read at many celebrations and festivities. During his period of illness Wulf still attended the weekly meetings of the Beth-El 2000 board of trustees

---

[31] *Zev Ben Shaul was Wulf Kahan's hebrew name and last name which literally means Wolf son of Saúl. The word Hakohen is a hebrew denomination used after a man's surname which indicates he is a direct descendant of the Cohanim (see footnote 29).*

[32] *Plurals for Bar and Bat-Mitzvah, celebrations for the boys and girls who become of age in the eyes of the community, on their thirteenth birthday for the former, and at twelve for the latter.*

with the same enthusiasm that always characterized him. At one of those meetings he confessed that having made those donations filled him with a very peculiar spiritual inner-peace: the Menorah represents light and the Torah shines on the ones who follow its principles. That is all part of the Spiritual Light to which he contributed with his generosity. The light is always there and when it glows it seems that his presence is there as well saying HINEYNI[33]."

The following words were written by Mr. Guillermo Torres Trueba C.:

FEELINGS FROM A PSALM...

"When facing death, man shakes his ability to live and humbly immerses himself in the space of ideas, of feelings, and of spirituality in a pleading search for answers and essential conceptions about which he inquires stutteringly, burdened by the pain and, sometimes, hurt by his pride."

"The shock that crushes a man's life when it comes to an end is a sign that should make us become more sensitive, authentically human, and willing to grasp incomparable beauty; not be satisfied with merely existing, but rather make that existence a complete enjoyment of spiritual abilities, the only ones that constitute human value."

"Wulf Kahan rests in the land of the just, that in which the rainbow is its endless horizon. He inhabits the mansions

---

[33] *Here I am.*

of light where it never gets dark; in the dwelling of those who sculpted the examples of universal self-improvement, for man like him cannot remain tied to ethic conceptions."

"If there is an epitaph for Wulf, it is the principle given by Dr. Hugo Bergmann: 'Will towards ethical actions.' Our dear friend made his life a permanent and warm source of love towards all that surrounded him: his family, his work, his hometown, his nation, and all noble cause; they were all embraced by the commitment of his affection and the conviction of his ideals."

"In Wulf, the thought by Maurice Samuel is a thesis: 'All Jews have to make a virtue out of necessity, for all beauty or dignity there is in life finds its origins in a necessity that was transformed into a virtue.' That is why he never stopped his transit through life -because a Jew does not feel harassed by life's limitations- and his nature, as Alfonso Pacífici once said, 'had a passionate tendency towards a better future, a better world, socially and politically."

"There are people that only become human after they have gone through adverse situations or suffered pain; Wulf made adversity, pain, and suffering become human."

"Before this life -Wulf's life- a group of people who loved him has wished to leave written testimony of the affection, admiration, and faith they felt for this man who now stands and confronts, with his indomitable love for life, all those who miss his physical presence. We probably still haven't learned the noble lesson that he taught on a daily basis: man lives what his works want him to, and his affection does not stop as he immerses himself in the meaning of his existence."

"Crying, then, means not being coherent with his teachings; walking holding his head up to the sun, without the blink caused by whining...that was his example."

"The people who write this abstract form part of the psalm of joy and hope that is sung by those who, like Wulf, do not let go of their shepherd's staff, and know they are only passers-by and never waste a road with weariness, indifference, or selfishness; there is only one road for them: the road of good!"

"Speaking through these paragraphs reflects the affection of a memory and the presence of a behavior in which the courage of living slakes its thirst with the only real source of peace in the human soul: love. The encounter with it means embracing Wulf, the man who made his spiritual peace public, especially by honoring the principles of the Mexican society, without ever forgetting the ancestral feeling that cradled his soul so he could be an example to his community, the Jewish community."

Dr. Jaime Laventman writes the following:
IN MEMORIAM. Adolfo Kahan.
"What is man?...What is man?"
"Duality born and maintained throughout life. Flesh and spirit; intentions and actions; dreams and realities."

"To 'Uncle Adolfo' -as we always used to call him- to his complete presence, his smile, appropriate for every situation, and his magnificent appearance which denoted the assurance he had within him knowing that he was the head of a whole family: he was their spokesman and their executor under the tactful canon law of a Jewish and secular education that supported all his actions. To the uncle who was near in those moments of decision, and to the on-hand advice he offered in those times of doubt or uncertainty. To the man we loved for having known how to combine in himself the figure of the husband and the father of his family group, and extending it to a whole life of social and community activity, thus proving that it is possible to experience the duality of being the head of a family and, on the other hand, being an example to all those who, at some point in their lives, had the chance to speak to him."

"A man of firm decisions based on his double sense of adventure and responsibility; an individual of actions with no hesitation, praised by some, questioned by others, but never hesitant, leaving to luck what he, in his stable mind, considered fair."

"He knew how to love and be loved by his own. Giving was more important than receiving, and listening was as vital as expressing a thought. Always surrounded by the incredible duality of life in itself, debating over what one believes and what must be done, over one's thoughts and one's actions. An example of integrity through a model life in which he, without a doubt, always played the role of the main character. However, he knew how to pass his principles on to the following generations that he forged, giving them not only an education to defend themselves with along their journey, but also firm foundations which would support them even during the toughest and angriest battles to come."

"A man of fast words whose look alone inspired trust and could make a stranger feel as a member of the family that he created with so much care."

"How wonderful it is for a man to be able to plant the most precious seed throughout his life and then harvest the fruit when strength has not abandoned him yet."

"What is man?...we ask ourselves during *Izcor*[34] and within our hearts we try to find the personal and lonely answer. And when we think of our own and see in their works the crystal of truth that time has polished with its endless patience, some of them stand out, some whose journey through life left teaching for others to follow. Uncle Adolfo was one of those people: positive duality in his actions and in his life, and most definitely, an example for all."

Mr. David Gorodzinsky says that "Wulf Kahan was a man with great charisma; he had become the boss to all of us around him."

"We followed him to Acapulco, to San Diego, to Miami, and well, anywhere he went...we would follow; all our lives revolved around him. The moment he was gone, Acapulco was over for us. Wulf was Acapulco."

---

[34] *Ceremony of remembrance of the dead.*

"He became someone indispensable in our lives with whom we needed to share everything that was important to us, all that was transcendent and, obviously, we enjoyed all the moments we spent with him, of which none were insignificant."

"He was born a leader and died a leader. Even in the difficult stage of his rehabilitation, he became a leader to other people that were being treated with therapy in the same place he was: he encouraged them to make their best effort. Although at that time he was incapacitated, he always tried to instill courage and energy in others. He always found a bright side to every bad thing, and he shared and celebrated all good things."

"I lived an experience with him in Miami after he had been through the operation: at first he didn't care much about sitting in the wheel chair, needing our help to get into the car and things like that. But then I was very impressed when on one occasion he didn't want anyone to help him into the car, so using his hands and making a very big effort -sweating and all- he managed to do it all by himself. He wanted to show us and, most of all, to prove himself -and he needed it- that he could do it on his own, that he did not always have to depend on others to accomplish things. He was a great person who in the end felt, in fact, the desire to die; but not because he had stopped loving life, on the contrary, he loved life and everything in it; he always expressed it through his incredible energy, his dynamic nature, and his actions in every moment of his life. That was why knowing that he was dependent on others was something he could not bear, that was what made him have a desire to die. He was in a good mood whenever he thought he might overcome the situation he was in; however, he became depressed when he lost hope of ever recovering from his illness, of being able to be independent again; it was then when he wished to die."

"It was a real challenge for him to go places where he had to go up a flight of stairs. Another thing that affected him a lot was that he could not always feed himself without any help: he needed someone to cut his meat and that made him have a very low self-esteem. He was a 'fighter' in every aspect and in the best sense of the word, that is, there was not a thing that he had set his mind on that he didn't accomplish. He was a warrior, dressed in tough garments but underneath he had the heart of a child."

Mr. Leopoldo Haces de la Fuente remembers Wulf Kahan during a conversation with his son Leopoldo Haces Abascal:

"Truthfully, I can tell you that I felt I could finally rest when he left us because I spent my days very concerned about him day and night knowing what he was going through. I know that wherever he may be, he too, realizes now that it was all for the best. There is not one day that passes by that I don't remember something we did. They were pleasant and indelible years the ones we spent together but I feel good that now it all remains in my mind and in my heart."

"Time flew right by us but I know that we made good use of it and we were lucky. You'll understand that we also told each other about unpleasant things that happened to us and almost all the time we both agreed on the solution. And when it wasn't like that, we would also let each other know, always respectfully and, most of all, very affectionately."

"I know better than anyone else what he went through in those last two years. I'm glad that the image of that Adolfo I always knew, full of life, is still fresh in my mind. The truth is that it was many, so many years ago that I don't remember well, but I think I met him somewhere around the year 1944. Of course, it is very hard for me to say what I always thought of him since we really treated each other with the love of two brothers."

"Anecdotes about him and with him, I have many, for together we attended a thousand parties, business meetings, funerals, weddings...any way, it was a whole life we spent together. Your godfather was a man who fought endlessly. As a husband he was truly the best; as a father, more than just an example. He was a respectful and very loving brother. I know my case is pretty unusual but with all his other friends -and he had many- he had a very affectionate relationship...he loved them and they loved him dearly."

"You know I've always liked giving examples because I believe that people understand better what I am referring to: I remember a time he tried and worked really hard to sell what I think was his first fleet of cars. He closed the deal with *Constructora Roshoff*, the company in charge of the construction of the Valsequillo dam around 1946. He sold them several dump trucks but it wasn't until they had ordered the vehicles that this problem began: he had to make a number of trips to Detroit so as to get the units."

"I know for a fact that facing the challenge that this represented was more important to him tan the money that would come from the deal. You see, in those times we were practically broke and money was pretty important to us, nevertheless, I am sure he got more satisfaction out of being successful in this business deal because, as you can probably imagine, there were many other people who wanted to make that transaction themselves. He ended up being friends -as it was expected of him- with all the company's engineers. We seldom had lunch with them back at the camp site they had put up in Guadalupe Victoria."

"Adolfo always had a special love for cars and the atmosphere of comradeship among the Chrysler dealers. It makes me sad to talk about that because those were some very good times for both of us..."

"When he decided to move to Mexico City and establish CIAMSA, I know he left a piece of his heart back in Puebla. But, I tell you, he was very plucky and he felt he was going to be more successful in the D.F. And all that he set his heart on, he accomplished."

"I felt sad to find out that he was moving to Mexico City, but we solved this quite easily because we both attended the AMDA meetings held on the street of Ejido, as well as the first *Automex Dealers Association* meetings. Then a long time later... remember?...we both had our condominiums in Acapulco. It was after that when he convinced me to buy the one over at the Acapulco Towers."

"Do you know what he used to do when we already had our apartments at the Acapulco Towers? He would stand out in his terrace garden at seven in the morning and would shout so I'd wake up and we could go to the beach together, to the yacht, to play golf, or any other place. Your godmother Estela would reprimand him about it and, so she wouldn't find out, he then changed his method and started throwing little pebbles at my window. He was untiring, he couldn't stay in one place for too long. He was always investigating where he could find a new place to have lunch at or go have fun in. He asked what new constructions there were in the port, who were the owners, how much they were worth, and well...it was a life full of nice things for him, except for the very end."

"I know that especially for him being in a wheel chair must have been worst than hell. The last times we had the opportunity to be together in Acapulco, when he was still in good shape, we visited Pichilingue one day and we dove off Paquito's sail boat...we laughed so much then..."

"I just remembered something really funny that happened to us when he had his yacht in Acapulco: he had invited some friends over to go out for a sail, have lunch, and visit the Roqueta island. We waited for them to arrive for a long time but they never showed up. We had already prepared the snack, bought roasted chickens and everything else. Suddenly, he turns around, he looks at me and says:"

'Buddy, what are we going to do with so many chickens?'

"Just imagine how gutsy he was... He once had to meet with Eloy Chouza to arrange everything about the site on Ejercito Nacional. He couldn't reach him anywhere and then he found out it was because Eloy was in Madrid. Well, what do you know...he just took the next flight out to Madrid and went looking for him. He was simply unbelievable, I tell you...nothing slipped by him!"

"Those conventions, which Raúl Tamayo still had the chance to attend, would be just like I used to tell Wulf: 'Buddy, they're going to think they went to Vietnam, not to a convention meant for resting.' He did the same thing, whether it was in Madrid, in Miami, or in Acapulco: we would be on the move all the time, from one place to another, and he would never get tired. Poor Estela... I don't know how she could always keep up with him. All of a sudden, he would disappear and I would ask her:

'Where is Adolfo?'
'He's making a phone call,' she would answer.

When he came back I would tell him 'Pal, did you start bothering Ari and Jack already? Leave them alone, they can handle it better than you can.'
'It's not what you think,' he'd say, 'I was just tempted to call.'

"I think I'll go on with the memories some other day, more calmly, because I'm getting too melancholic now..."

These words were said by Rabbi Marcelo Rittner as he bid Wulf Kahan farewell: "I can say that he's a figure that leaves a mark that not even time can erase. Since my arrival in Mexico I always had a very close relationship with Wulf and Estela, his wife. When they celebrated their gold wedding anniversary, I was responsible of presiding the ceremony where they renewed their wedding vows. It was a very moving and beautiful event. Wulf was especially the image of a man whose family was the core of his life."

"Sometime someone said that 'there is a part of us that never dies,' that part for which we work all our life, that we plan; the footprints we leave on the road of life; that is the part of us that stays with humanity forever. Don Wulf leaves indelible footprints on that road. His behavior, his actions, his footsteps, his life, they were all a blessing; his memory will be one, as well."

"Someone said one time that we should never ask:

'How did he die?...but rather how did he live?'
'How much did he earn?...but rather how much did he give?'

"These are the parameters that measure the value of a man's life as a human being."

"Do not ask:
'What were his beliefs or which was his sanctuary?...but rather if he helped the people who needed him.'

"Do not ask:

'What did the papers say about his passing?...but rather how many people grieve about his death?'

"In the eyes of society, Wulf was an example of honesty; in the eyes of the community, he was a man dedicated to the most noble ideals; in the eyes of the congregation, an engine and a model of faith; in the eyes of his family, a beautiful human being, a companion for life; and for his rabbi and many other people, a great friend."

"Those were the parameters of Wulf's life: ideals, faith, friendship, perseverance. How will we remember him?... As a man with qualities that exceeded his defects; we will remember him with the responsibility of continuing his work and completing his dreams."

Before we come to the end of this 'road', Jack, Wulf Kahan's youngest son, has written the following words:

"Sitting in front of the fireplace, I find myself remembering so many very intense moments that I spent with my father throughout 38 years.

It is a deep feeling that which fills my eyes with tears every time that, so easily, I remember how much I loved him. At the same time, I realize that when remembering him I feel my soul fill up with emotion and it makes me value more all that surrounds me. It's the faith in the principles that he knew how to pass on to me that gives me the strength to understand that he is no longer here.

Remembering him is not something difficult for me to do, it is more like an automatic feeling that pops into my mind with such power that it is only possible to be experienced by someone who has lost a person like him. He was a person that, besides from giving me life along with my mother, gave me the strength for my existence; he taught me to love God and life.

Before talking about my father, I would like to refer to my mother. Yes, that lady that, with her intelligence and her love for her husband, knew how to be a model woman, showing her children and the world how she gave him, her husband, her support at any time. Always dignified and elegant, always self-assured and calm, although the pain inside may never stop.

So many times we stood there, dazzled by my father's strong nature, by his perseverance and effort, by his honesty and love. Nevertheless, she was always, always there, preparing him to face any challenge, as difficult as it might be. Fighting side by side all the time, guiding their children along a path of good health and respect. Picturing my dad without my mom is like looking at him with just one eye.

Now, mom, when it's time for you to walk through the rest of your life without him, I can tell you, just a few months after his death, how little he knew about you and how proud of you we all are. As always, you have given us the example of the way to face this situation like only you know how; with the courage and determination, with the love and unbreakable faith that you show every time you stand up to say *Kaddish*[35] with us.

It is a world of experiences that surround my life and my relationship with my father, to whom I dedicated all my efforts, my self-improvement, and my triumphs. He was always there: when I had to stand up for what I believed in, telling me the things that were on his mind but always in an elegant manner, with his blessing and his support, and at the end he would always say: do whatever you decide.

Over and over again he helped me see things more clearly, he taught to think on long-term basis, to base my decisions on myself and my family; a family that he helped me choose when he encouraged me to marry Tita. We talked one whole night about it. Maybe that was the most inten e night of my life, since my mom was away on a trip and he dedicated his time and mind to me, to the point that he asked me in such simple words as 'Do you love her?' to which I answered yes. 'Would you like her to be the mother of your children?' and again I said yes. 'Then what are you waiting for to marry her?'

Daddy, now I can say thanks... because you were not wrong, because if I had to choose all over again now, after sixteen years of marriage and three children later, I would pick the same woman.

---

[35] *Prayer of mourning that is said by the male sons of the deceased during the morning and evening religious services, every day for a period of eleven months.*

My father let me be, although that always brought along discussions about how I had to behave. There were many times that we argued and argued to the point that we even challenged one another. He used to tell me about the way that he had established his business, how he had arrived from Russia, how they had managed to survive in Mexico, and how hard he had worked to accomplish something in his life. But when he realized that it was already ten o'clock at night and he had not convinced me, and the phone would ring and it was my mom calling, then he would say 'tomorrow will be another day.'

There were times when we had different points of view about something and I noticed that his face would turn red during the discussion; when he could not convince me about whatever he was saying, he would come home and tell my mom what had happened and that I had not even paid attention to him.

However, always, every time that the situation would get red-hot, he would approach me the next day and ended up telling me:

'It's just that you and I have the same character.'
Maybe it was that attitude of his that helped me face life with courage. Daddy, now that you are not here, I'm so lucky to be able to thank God that the apple did not fall too far from the tree and I am very proud to be your own seed.

I remember that time when I lived in San Diego and you asked me if I had thought it through after having lived abroad for five years; if I had no desire of moving back to

Mexico, because you missed my children more than you missed me. What happened is that you already knew what buttons to push: you wanted me to get all anxious and think about how selfish I had been not to let my children spend more time with their grandparents, their uncles and aunts, their cousins, and with so many other Mexicans like them, and about all that we would miss out on if we did not come back to Mexico.

As always, you made me reflect on an important aspect of my life and you gave me the time to make a decision. I must confess that you were not mistaken, for my wife and children remember fondly every minute that they ever spent with you, and now that you have left us they thank you for having made us come back.

Dad, since you left I close my eyes wishing I could find you and I ask myself where have you gone and what have you found in that far away place. I remember that when I was my children's age and you left on a trip I would wait restlessly for you to come back and see what presents you had brought me and the pictures you had taken. Today, thanks to all the photos you took, the family, all gathered, has seen and remembered all those beautiful moments, and we have realized that the only thing that is constant in life is change: some fat, others skinny. There's no doubt whatsoever that in each one of these photos you reflected the image of the person you wanted to be: completely transparent, with an enormous love for your wife, your family, your children, and your friends. You taught that the world lies within our reach if only we try hard enough, and that all people, no matter what nationality or religion, were your friends; you taught us to respect and love them.

I do not hold many memories of the times when I was a little boy since you always wanted to see me as a young man: you taught me to ski before teaching me how to swim; to dance before teaching me how to sing; to work before teaching me how to multiply. I thank you so very much for having given me the opportunity of working not only with you, but also with my brother, my uncle, and my cousin. I remember the first time you grabbed me I was barely fourteen years old and you had told me that business was not going well and that you needed me to help you in the afternoons and during vacations. You made me feel so important...

You trusted me; you left me in charge of the business every time you went out on a trip. You would always call me on the phone and ask me if there had been any action, until I finally understood that all the action that there could ever be in the business would never be enough to keep you happy.

I remember you liked to wake me up in the mornings so you could take me with you to work and when we arrived at the office, I would show you an invoice full of mistakes or I would make a comment about an upset client. You would then call the department manager on duty and in two minutes you showed him what was wrong and I would say to myself: that's my daddy.

How proud I felt when I used to put on your neck ties, or your shoes, or wear your lotions, or go with you here and there to meet with important people. I felt so proud to look all around me and feel that I was a very loved and respected person. I will never forget the times when you smoked your pipe and left behind a scent of cherry tobacco. I remember you liked drinking whisky and soda, watching the girls go by, but what excited you the most was taking your yacht out for a sail.

Your yacht, the 'Sea Wulf'... I remember that day when I saw you arrive from Los Angeles with your 31 ft. Chris-craft and wearing your captain hat. That day you looked as if you had won the jackpot thanks to your perseverance and effort in the world of business: I witnessed how your wife was changing right before my eyes and you were turning into a sea wolf. You invited everyone you saw to come visit your yacht.

You would tell my mom:

'Estela, what are you worried about? We have cheese and sausages.' But you would always see her arrive at the yacht with some *ceviche*[36] and miniature chicken tacos. You would prepare the sausage and we would all enjoy its smell. Do you remember Chirimillas, our first boatman, dad? We spent so many moments on board that yacht! Every time you bought a new boat you always remembered to bring me a miniature fishing boat or a pair of tiny water-skis with my name on them. Do you remember when we used to ski together, both of us at the same time, and one time

---

[36] *Typical Mexican fish cocktail which recipe was created originally in the port of Acapulco.*

we crashed into each other while crossing the wake and I nearly had to pull you out of the water by the hair? I thought you were going to kill me for it. But every thing was fun and games if we were in the sea. The bigger the waves, the faster we would go. You taught me how to overcome my fear of the sea and to control your yacht all by my self: how to bring it in and pull out from the docks, how to raise the anchor, how to moor the yacht, how to sail it and enjoy it.

Remember the time you woke me up at seven AM, after I had gotten home from the disco just a few hours before, so we could go buy new anchors for the boat? I knew you did not need new anchors because you already had them, but that was your way of preventing that I go out partying every night.

You always liked being mischievous. That was how you had the most fun and my mom would just sigh 'Oh, Adolfo!'; but those were the moments when I felt I loved you the most.

When we are kids, we are always showing off 'look at how old my dad is and how young he looks!' Daddy, I met you when you were really not that young anymore; when I was born you were already 40 years old -that's why they call me 'the fluke'. This is something I would have never imagined, having so many moms and dads...Ari always thought of me as a son, and so did Ruthy and Perla. Boy, was I lucky! Everyone would just mistake me for their child.

It's Sunday today, we are only three days away from Yom Kippur, your birthday. I told Ari that I had dreamed about you and that in my dream you had told me where you were, how things were going for you, and what you had seen there. You made me remember the times when we used to sit and chat about your trips, your illusions, your accomplishments, and your frustrations.

I really wanted to see you at the temple, sitting beside us asking God for one year more. Dad, I truly missed you this time; this year I had to stay in the synagogue the whole service because you were not there anymore. Where were you? What were you doing? Didn't you remember what congregation you belonged to?... No daddy, I know we are not going to argue anymore, that there is no time left for disagreements or celebrations; no more photos. We already said good-bye that rainy day; that day against which you fought so much, so much; that day in which God embraced he who loved life from his first day; that young man who died old; that man who always spoke his mind; my father, who lived happily almost all his life.

As the flame in the fireplace goes out, but not so the one in my heart, I wish you a good night, daddy.

Your son, Jack."

The heavens started to become tinted with light; the first rays of sun appeared in the horizon. I had spent the whole night awake; we had buried my father the previous afternoon. I wrote him this letter:

"May 29, 1992.
Dad,

This morning at dawn I start to reflect on your departure.

I swear it caught me by surprise for, in spite of having spent these last few fears with you, I was never aware that your farewell was so close.

Above all, I ask you to forgive me for not being with you during the moments of your boarder crossing, nevertheless, I'm sure that your re-encounter with God was magnificent. I hope you were able to confirm that He never left your side; it was rather that you had one last mission to carry out on this land that you loved so and in which your memory grows with every moment that passes by.

I will live eternally grateful that you kept me company during my presidential period at the AMDA. I never had any doubts that I could help you during your difficult illness and that it would give me the courage and responsibility you always wanted us to acquire. I'm certain that without your inspiration and support I would have never been able to play a role that would satisfy you. Your advice was always received with love: THANK YOU; DADDY; FOR YOUR SUPPORT.

Only a few hours after your departure the fog in my eyes starts to fade away and I can see, feeling enormously peaceful, that your journey in this world leaves an indelible mark of THE MAN WHO ALWAYS LOVED LIFE AND FELT GRATEFUL TOWARDS IT. If at some point you told us that you wanted to die, it was because you felt your job here was done and you were tired. Now that you must be feeling better about yourself, certain that your self-esteem is again what it used to be, and that your faith and love for God are the same as they were, He will let us rescue the image we had always had of you. Your great and best friend, Fernando Katz, was telling me yesterday after your burial that he had never experienced such a worthy and crowded farewell.

Daddy, I swear I was also shocked at the number of people who came to bid you farewell. Everyone commented that you were a man who loved life and knew how to experience it to its maximum, but most of all, they all mentioned that you let others learn to live and enjoy life by your side.

Your dear friend Leopoldo Haces decided that he should come to your burial when he found out about your passing. This pleased me very much, but at the same time I felt somewhat sorry because you would have liked him to visit you while you were still alive; that was your wish. Nevertheless, I now understand, because of the love he always showed for you, that he did not want to hurt you, he was afraid he might hurt your feelings; that is why I now know that, when you died, there was no possibility of watching you in a state you never wanted people to see you in: as a MAN who inspired pity and compassion; shouting 'THE SHOW'S OVER, I'M DONE, I WANT TO DIE'...words, daddy, that only now I am beginning to understand.

I MISS YOU VERY MUCH, but it comforts me to know that you are happy about having taken the most important step, the definite one that would leave the deepest mark any FATHER could leave in his son's being.

If we were able to choose parenthood, I would have chosen yours.

DADDY, changing the subject, you must feel very proud of your companion: my MOM. With every moment that passes by, leaving your death behind in time, she behaves as she always has, as your eternal admirer and devoted companion, and the scenes of anger and disagreements that you lived during your long convalescence are now being forgotten. Her beautiful, strong, and most of all, loving personality shelters us once more; her authentic and firm decision to continue the physical and moral home that both of you founded, which could have crumbled now that you're gone, emerges like an enormous mountain of love carved and sculptured with the patina of time. MY RESPECTS TO THIS QUIET WOMAN THAT LIVES HER DESTINY WITH ABNEGATION AND LOVE.

DADDY, please say hello to all our dear ones who must be greeting you very affectionately, for they were already awaiting your arrival fore some time, and I'm sure that they were praying for your journey to be a fast and easy one.

Your son, Ari.

P.S. DEAR LORD, I THANK YOU FOR LETTING ME BORROW YOUR DEAR SON WULF FOR TWO YEARS AND TWO MONTHS MORE. I THANK YOU FOR

HAVING PREPARED US GRADUALLY FOR HIS FINAL DEPARTURE. BUT I THANK YOU THE MOST FOR MAKING HIM MY FATHER, PHYSICALLY DURING ALMOST 55 YEARS, AND MAKING HIM ETERNALLY MY PROGENITOR, GRANDFATHER OF MY CHILDREN, AND GREAT-GRANDFATHER OF MY GREAT-GRANDCHILDREN. YOU HAVE DISTINGUISHED US AMONG YOUR CREATION AND WE STAND IN DEBT WITH YOU FOR IT."

Jack, Wulf, and Ari Kahan.

Epilogue

And at last, freedom

"Freedom, Sancho, is one of the most precious gifts that Heaven has bestowed upon men; no treasures that earth holds buried or the sea conceals can compare with it; for freedom, as for honor, life may and should be ventured; and on the other hand, captivity is the greatest evil that can fall to the lot of man." (Miguel de Cervantes Saavedra)[37]

It is possible that Wulf Kahan wanted to venture his life in search of freedom. He knew for a fact that "captivity is the greatest evil that can fall to the lot of man" and knew that his body did not respond any longer.

Nevertheless, he never gave up. Ever since the beginning of his illness, he knew that he was facing a new challenge and that he had to wage that battle in order to be an example to the people who loved him. However, from the start he was aware that with his illness he was setting out on a new journey, a journey different from the ones he had been through before; it was the one that would lead him to eternal freedom.

[37] *See footnote 30*

Thanks

This book would not have been possible without the generous collaboration of the following people:

Federico Anaya Sánchez
Agustín Arriaga Rivera
Vicente Ariztegui Perochea
Vito Bellifémine Grech
Gilberto Cantú Gottwald
María de Lourdes Cárdenas de Gil
Irma Carrillo Zapata
Javier Castellanos Fuentes
Fernando Castro Rodríguez
Fernando Cohen Fis
Samy Cohen Oved
Norberto Cortés Suárez
Jorge Cheirif
Benjamín Cheirif Derzavich
Michelle Cheirif Derzavich
Saul Delgado Rodríguez
Heidy Derzavich Kahan
Fernando Derzavich Gurvich
Arie Derzavich Kahan
Jack Derzavich Kahan
Samy Derzavich Kahan
Jorge Dillman A.
Sergio Domínguez Vargas
Carlos Doring Hermosillo
Mario Duque Pozen
Teresa Edid de Kahan
Jaime Edid Laham
Gustavo Escobar Montes
Mossy Farca de Kahan
Eduardo Luis Feher
Hernán Figueroa Cal y Mayor
César Flores E.
Estela Freund de Kahan
Daniel Gancz Kahan

Gabriela Gancz Kahan
Jaime Gancz Kahan
Sandra Gancz Kahan
José Gancz Loshak
Diego Garibay García de Quevedo
Jorge Garibay Romanillos
Miguel Angel Gil Corrales
Daniel González D'Bejarle
Laura González Flores
David Gorodzinsky Miller
Isaac Grabinski Ash
Salo Grabinski Steider
Pablo Guerra Compean
Leopoldo Haces Abascal
Leopoldo Haces de la Fuente
Jim Hedges
Ana Rosa Hernández López
José Hernández Patrón
Raquel Huber de Kahan
Leibele Jinich
Miguel Jusidman
Perla Kahan de Derzavich
Ruthy Kahan de Gancz
Patricia Kahan de Wertman
Alexander Kahan Edid
Gabriel Kahan Edid
Katiana Kahan Edid
Luis Kahan Elperin
Jack Kahan Freund
Anna Kahan Grabinski
Carlos Kahan Grabinski
Saul Kahan Grabinski
Samuel Kahan Shapiro
Alejandro Kahan Sorokin
Fernando Katz Avruzky
Carlos A. Kretschmer
Antonio Laguna Herrera
Jaime Lavetman G.
Jesús Licona Manríquez
Alberto Liz Fabre

Alberto López de Nava
Alberto Lozano de la Vega
Guillermo Maldonado León
Jorge Maldonado Romero
José Mangino
Francisco Javier Miranda M.
Agustín Ochoa Mayo
Juan José Ortega Espinoza
Jorge Orvañanos Lascurain
Eduardo Orvañanos Zúñiga
Arturo Pérez Gutiérrez
Francisco Plancarte Haro
Mauricio Rioseco Orihuela
Marcelo Rittner
Saul Rosales Contreras
Fernando Rosas Pantaleón
Carlos Rossell Alvarez
Emilio Sánchez Peláez
Raya Shapiro de Kahan
Christian Schjetnan Garduño
Beny Schoenfeld Modiano
Oscar Siegal Flattau
Irene Sorokin de Kahan
Philip Steinberg
Francisco Torrado Haza
Guillermo Torres Trueba C.
Agustín Velasco Korndoffer
Manuel Viniegra Zubiria
Werner Gunnar
Bernardo Wertman Braun
Janisse Wertman Kahan
Tali Wertman Kahan
Roberto Zapata Gil

To all of them, once again, thanks!

Appendix

I never thought that the book **Wulf Kahan, my Father** was going to be accepted with so much affection. I was not expecting to cause such a positive reaction in other human beings by having honored the figure of the father.

Ever since the presentation of this book, on December 1st, 1992, I have received a lot of letters, telephone calls, messages, and comments regarding this work of Wulf Kahan's personality.

Although I knew he had had numerous friends, I never imagined that there were so many people who had loved my father.

In this appendix, that I add to the third and fourth editions of the book, I want to express my gratitude for all the shows of affection and the ideas conveyed. With them I can now embellish the work.

All of them extremely valuable, all close to my heart. I have been saving the messages as they have been reaching me and in that same order I present them here.

Being always limited by space, it is not possible for me to reproduce the texts in their complete versions; nor can I include the words of all the people who have showed me their respect and appreciation.

To all, thank you very much.

"The Kahan family is like my family to me; I share their happiness as well as their sorrow. Don Wulf Kahan: we will always remember him as an honest man and a model of continuity for many families."

Susy Leipuner

"Mr. Wulf taught me what a true family is. After my father's death I was able to understand what my mother and siblings felt, give them my sincere and unconditional support, and I realized the unrestrained affection that our neighbor and friend Wulf always showed for us. For me, he has not died because he lives in the hearts and minds of all those who knew him. I thank the Lord for having given me the opportunity to meet this wonderful family and I would like them to know that my family and I love them dearly."

Javier Mendoza Valdez

"Through the book, we could verify Wulf Kahan's human quality. We could also sense the importance of this just, fair, charismatic man and forerunner of a concept of total quality in the business world."

Jaime and Minny Arbitman

"Wulf Kahan, a man gifted by destiny with a road few have taken, one to which he cleaved and, at the same time, one he bequeath onto many others for them to walk on."

Antonio Villagrán Polo

"I have read the whole book and I realized that it contains a very moving and exemplary story for any

Mexican who wishes to follow that road or path that Mr. Adolfo Kahan paved from beginning to end.

Mr. Ari Kahan, since I did not have the honor of meeting Mr. Wulf alive, I realize that having read a part of his lifetime history, now, it seems as if I had spent some time with him. That book shows key steps one should follow in order to be successful in any business one wishes to start.

Apart from the triumphs and accomplishments achieved by Mr. Wulf, I was surprised to find out how he managed to keep his family together, and learn to live with and help his fellow men without asking for anything in return.

That is why the Mexican people should feel proud of having had in our country a man that, without having been born here, made his best effort and fought for the well-being of many people when he created a job source as is *Kahan Automotriz*.

I believe that if everyone read the contents of this book, they would realize that Mr. Wulf was a person who worked hard to keep Mexico's name as high as he possibly could in the automotive industry. This is the reason why many Mexican entrepreneurs should and must follow the example set by Mr. Wulf.

Just as he believed in Mexico, all his family and all his staff kept on going and believed in him, as well.

Mr. Ari, all his friends and workers will continue to count on you and believe in you."

Julián Hector García

"The book reveals Wulf Kahan's nature: alive until the end; never gave up. It's a privilege for me to share these feelings with his family."

Jorge Leipuner

"An entire book has not been enough to continue talking about Don Adolfo. He has left an indelible mark on all of us who knew him and loved him.

Doña Estela, Ari, Perlita, Ruthy, Jackie: we congratulate you for having a husband and a father that was a model for others to follow and we envy you, in the good sense of the word, for having had the opportunity to spend so many unforgettable moments with Don Wulf the way you did.

Nevertheless, we feel honored and flattered to have been able to enjoy the times we shared with Don Adolfo, which never were nor will be enough. Let us follow his example and cultivate our friendship even more."

Francisco Torrado Haza

"The hearts and souls of Wulf Kahan and Federico Rioseco started a beautiful friendship that can now be enjoyed by their future generations. Congratulations!"

Blanca Orihuela de Rioseco

"Ari Kahan has spilled all his sensitivity and all his feelings of filial love onto the pages of this book so as to rise the most magnificent monument as a tribute to his beloved father.

Neither stone, nor marble, nor bronze can compare to the memories, always alive, always latent, in the pages that form part of a work meant to glorify the figure of a loved one.

Ari Kahan deserves all the admiration possible for he has revealed himself as an extraordinary son who launched himself into the noble task of examining, through his own and others' experiences, the great dimension of Wulf Kahan's soul. Thus, he went out in search for opinions that let him discover unknown facets, aspects of his father's life that he maybe suspected and now, like rays of light on a mirror, they become surprising reflections of a charismatic personality of captivating humane tonality.

From the most humble people to the most opulent personalities that offered their ideas about the book's main character, Wulf Kahan, who they knew through a family, social, labor, or business relationship, they all helped create a monument of love from son to father.

Now, Ari has full knowledge of the greatness within his father's persona, one that he suspected since he was a child, and what could be better than to translate that image onto a book that would be perennial testimony of the existence of a man which would prove useful to society.

Every time the pages of this work, written from the heart, are opened, Wulf Kahan will come to life again with all the might in his spirit, a spirit which conjugated the qualities of an extraordinary entrepreneur with the ones of a great human being.

Honoring Wulf Kahan is also honoring his beloved wife, Estela. That is why Ari did not forget to include in his pages the generous and unselfish mother that knew how to be the ideal companion, who traveled with Wulf down the road of life and shared with him his hours of joy and sorrow, his difficult moments and his triumphs, being always his support and the guiding light at home.

...Despite his illness, Wulf Kahan continued being as honest, dignified, and energetic as ever before. I remember when Ari used to take him to the synagogue in his wheel chair and affectionately helped him stand up for the

Ahmidah[38] and they both listened to the religious chants. And, in those sublime moments, his eyes seemed to prepare for his encounter with God, praying for his family to continue receiving the gifts that he so generously had provided for them during his existence."

Manuel Levinsky

"I have just received, through Mrs. Anita Viskin and the *Amigos Mexicanos de la Universidad Hebrea de Jerusalem*[39] organization, your book of memories that outline the dynamic figure of your father, Wulf-Adolfo.

This document, somewhat personal and familiar, has moved me deeply. The details about Adolfo Kahan's social and commercial activity carry a testimony about the environment, both Jewish and gentile, of the several stages of his life, with which this small tome stops being the Kahan's personal patrimony and becomes an available source of information for all historians."

Haim Avni

"As it happens with all good things, I will surely learn something from your father's book."

Arturo Pérez Gutiérrez

---

[38] *Jewish prayer, also called the Shmoneh-esreh (which means eighteen), that forms a part of the morning, afternoon, and evening prayers and in which Jewish people say eighteen prayers to thank God for different things.*

[39] *Mexican Friends of the Hebrew University of Jerusalem.*

"As I read the book, I felt Adolfo's presence at all times and lived the memories of a life full of friendship."

Bertha Belkind

"On the same day that you sent me the book, in the afternoon I had to leave on a business trip to Dallas, Texas and it had been many years since I have had such an extraordinary travel companion as was your book.

I would like to express in a few words the great emotion and deep gratitude I feel for the work regarding your dear father, Wulf Kahan, as well as my respect and admiration for the exemplary union among all your family."

Javier Martínez Salinas

"All of us that were Wulf Kahan's friends could feel a little bit of that joy for living that only a few people have and which characterized Adolfo during his whole life."

Jaime Toiber

"Our friendship was a very short one. I was amazed by his strength and likeableness. He was very charismatic and I would have loved to continue seeing him. I'm sorry that he had to leave us so soon."

Daniel Rubinsky

"Thank you, Ari, for giving me the opportunity of living your joys and sorrows with you. Thank you for showing your affection towards us when we too have experienced moments of sorrow or joy."

Elena V. de Mendoza

"This book has made me think of death not as an end, for your father's spirit still lives within all of you and the people who had the pleasure of knowing him. Thank you so much for sharing these experiences with us."

Matilde Sandoval de Villagra

"Thank, Ari, because I discovered a new feeling in life which I don't know how to call. As you well have said: first, I thank God and then I thank for your existence and for you having given me lovely moments.

I would like to be a great-grandfather like Wulf, and a grandfather like Ari.

I would like to be a grandfather like Wulf, and a father like Ari.

I would like to be a father like Wulf, and a son like Ari.

I would like to be a person like Wulf and Ari.

I thank you, Ari. It has been an ineffable lesson about like for all of us who appreciate it. May God continue blessing all your family."

Hector Herrera

"Building a family is one of the most important things for parents. Surely, your father, wherever he may be, must feel very, very proud of you. It is a legacy which will forever remain in the soul of all the Kahan family."

Raquel and Abraham Edvabny

"The object of the book reflects the quality of Ari Kahan's spirit and his positive and successful view of life which irradiates physical and moral greatness."

Beatriz Sanabria

"Today I finished reading the marvelous book you were so kind to give me as a present. I wanted to call you, but my emotion is so great that I knew I wasn't going to be able to tell you what my heart felt...

Now I tell you that the book, which is a tribute to your father, has filled me with emotion; with it I have learned more than I could ever learn in many years of life. You and him are all an example to be followed. The human beings that leave a mark of loyalty, dignity, love and respect, never die: the stay in the hearts of each of their loved ones and of the people that had the honor of meeting them. The letter you write to your father at the end of the book made me think about the great respect and admiration I had for my own father. I must confess that I have cried with emotion and that this book is not only a tribute to your father: it is a handbook for day to day life, for whoever wants to be the best and the greatest in what is known as leading a full life. Few are the people who have the privilege and the heart like the one your marvelous father had, and in consequence, like the one his children, grandchildren, and great-grandchildren have, as well. It was only a few times that I so him with your mom, a beautiful woman and a lady in every sense of the word. Your daddy is not gone: he lives in everyone of you."

Ana Elena Abuasale

"Let me tell you, Ari, that your book titled *Wulf Kahan, my Father* is a very valuable testimony of the life led by this model Mexican entrepreneur, in its various facets: as a man, as a patriarch, as a citizen committed to his society and to the moment in history in which he lived."

Gilberto Borja Navarrete

"I congratulate you, Ari, on the family nucleus that Wulf Kahan created. I admire the richness of the moral values that he passed on to you. And talking about passing on, I sensed clearly that it is now your turn to inherit the central place he had in the life of the Kahan family. What a big responsibility this will be for you!"

Luis Porteny

"We received a copy of the book *Wulf Kahan, my Father* that you so kindly sent to our library at the *Centro Deportivo Israelita*, and we are sure it will prove very useful to all our readers."

Raquel Strauss

"I am certain that in the book I will find many of the thoughts and attitudes that have let us feel identified with each other. I wish you, Ari, that success in business never end, but especially that the spiritual peace you transmit keep on growing."

Luis G. Cárcoba G.

"Having the necessity of expressing my feelings, I will put aside all formalism. It's so tough when you lose a person that is dear to you, isn't it? When you pass through the different stages of life and suddenly lose one of your parents, the thought which comes to mind is that law of nature is being fulfilled, that it is something we all have to go through, that maybe time will cure the wounds, but I don't believe it is so.

It is a wound that will never be cured in the heart, for even if you show the opposite, the pain will be there for the rest of our days.

What is more important is to transmit on to our descendants the memories that, in our case, prove as very proud of our parents: Wulf and Jacobo, model fathers in every sense of the word. Ari, how can I find the words to express the deep respect and admiration I feel for you, for the friendship, the pride, and most of all the respect that you so completely showed for your father all throughout your relationship with him, which, as you said, will never end.

Every time I saw you with him, a certain envy -good envy- would form inside me for I didn't have enough time to tell or show my father just how much I loved him, how much I admired him, how much I wanted to hug him long and hard and feel him near again; never the less, I believe our relationship goes on and will go on eternally.

This will be possible by loving Paty and my children in the same way that your father and mine loved us, and transmit to them what is really essential in life: always believe in God and be a good human being."

Bernardo "Berele" Wertman

"All of us, the people who knew Don Wulf and learned to appreciate his human sensitivity, respectfully share this well-deserved tribute."

Juan Manuel Arriaga

"I'm very glad to have a friend that is capable of writing such valuable and realistic ideas about his father. Although I didn't have the chance to know Wulf Kahan by sharing experiences with him, I have gotten to know some aspects about his personality, his appeal, and many other qualities through the amazing anecdotes you include in your work."

Carlos Llano

"Spiritually moved, I was able to relive important moments that left a mark in his life, enjoying the wonderful presence of the objective maker himself."

Manuel Arriaga Quintana

"I had the luck and the honor of meeting your father a few months before his death. I was a witness to his effort and determination to make it, on his own two feet, to the convention where you were handing over the AMDA presidency; and I could see how he reached his goal before the applause and admiration of more than a thousand entrepreneurs in the automotive industry. What you have done is the most beautiful tribute to his memory. It is materializing, now it is becoming real. As the Taj-Mahal signified a monument of the love a man felt for a woman, thus your book is the monument of the love of a son for his father. With it you fully obey the spirit and writing of the Fourth Commandment, which is the first commandment with a reward: *Thou shall honor thy father and thy mother and a good and long life shall fall onto thee.*"

Gustavo Serrano

"Ari, I thank you enormously for sending me your book, *Wulf Kahan, my Father*, which you recently published. I congratulate you on this work that helps us to get to know the daily life of this country -so deteriorated nowadays-through the presence of a family of immigrants who arrived in Mexico in 1922. It has a splendid literary style and I found it very interesting."

Manuel Ramos Medina

"On behalf of the *Comité Israelita de México*[40] and through these lines we warmly and courteously congratulate you on the book titled *Wulf Kahan, my Father*...We wish you the achievement of greater success in the road which you have paved with the moral values and the principles of our tradition."

Simón Nissan R. And Moisés Punsky

"Thank you -from the depths of our hearts- for the beautiful book *Wulf Kahan, my Father*, honoring a great man, Wulf Kahan. A person who started two legends: an amazing family and an extraordinary business. As our *Sabra*[41] children say: *Kol Ha'kvod* (my utmost respects)."

Devorah and Eliezer Rafaeli

"Receive our best regards and congratulations on the book, excellent homage you put together for your father."

Hector Fernández Rousselon

"What better tribute to a father than putting his life in a book. Man leaves this world and his works remain."

Jacobo and Susana Leifshitz

---

[40] *The organization which represents the Jewish community before the Mexican society.*
[41] *Israeli*

"Congratulations, Ari. A touching occasion to pay homage to your father, who left a deep mark of his friendship and human values in all of us, his friends."

Alfonso Castillo Saldaña

"The best tribute is leading your life with bravery; the life that, from his, Wulf passed on to you. Undoubtedly, he will forever be present through his family from generation to generation."

Alberto and Sara Lozano

"If I felt proud to be working for you before this, now, I feel proud and happy."

Fernando San Miguel

"I think it is marvelous for a person to not forget and honor his parents and then share it with his friends. The good seed Ari planted with this book will give wonderful fruits that will feed his good soul."

Jorge Fastlich

"I received and took in the book *Wulf Kahan, my Father*, feeling each word of it with immense profoundness. Ari, I congratulate you on your work."

Manuel Martínez Domínguez

"Motivated by the emotion that came with reading your book, I want to express my gratitude, Mr. Ari, for giving me the opportunity to get to know your father more and to somehow be able to become closer to you.

I am very glad about having read the story of such an important man and, most of all, about having the chance to know him and witness his character and how his presence reflected his dominant nature.

"I have one reproach against time, though, for it didn't let me thank Mr. Wulf for having created a person such as you, who has trusted me and, above all, has shared the fruits of his hard work not only with me but also with every one of my work mates, giving us all the opportunity of growing by his side.

Also, having you as my witness, I want to thank the Lord for giving me the chance of working here and helping me find a boss who I can talk with, not only about the things regarding our work, but also about personal matters."

Janet Gil

"The people who talk in your book let me know who your father was and the moral values he had, something I really had a hunch about when I met you. If he was capable of creating a son such as yourself, a fine example of what a son should be... I don't think anyone could feel more satisfied. You will always touch my heart whenever I hear you sing *Mi Viejo* for I still do not have enough serenity within me do to it myself."

Alfonso González Karg

"Congratulations, Ari, on the extraordinary work in which you compiled such important passages of your father's life. This is an exemplary act, worthy of being imitated by many other people."

Jesús Martínez Celada

"Yesterday I finished reading you book, *my Father*, and I realize that I didn't have the opportunity of meeting a man as extraordinary as was Wulf Kahan, but I am in deed very lucky to consider you -that inherited many of his virtues- as one of my friends.

On the other hand, I must tell you that the book has made me reflect on certain aspects of my life which I hope someday I can comment with you. Placing this book in my hands is one more of the many things I have to thank you for."

Luis Martínez G.

"Apart from being a very interesting biography, your book is a tribute paid to an extraordinary man, who inculcated tenacity and effort in his family; the mentality and strength that form part of the Kahan family and that, in its transcendence, became very well-known to others."

Aurelio Borgaro Mills

"Sitting calmly sometime around the first few days of the year, with a view of the bay of Acapulco, I finished reading the last page of the book *Wulf Kahan, my Father*.

It was a coincidence that I was in Acapulco when I was able to devote myself to reading this book about fragments of your father's life. There were many coincidences with a lot of things that my father tell me about his youth: son of Lebanese immigrants; he started out selling fabric in the downtown area and then invested his capital on importing two automobiles, which he then sold in Mexico.

As I was reading the book I was able to awaken the memory of how difficult it had been for them to start out back in those days, according to my father's anecdotes.

Thank you, Ari, for giving me that opportunity. And thanks, as well, for having expressed the importance of family and of honesty between father and son.

Congratulations on your hard work, but above all, on having had the father you did."

Jorge S. Tame Ayub

"Thanks so much, dear Ari, for your note and your book about your father, Wulf. I was very sorry to hear about his death. I offer you and your family my deepest sympathies."

Robert A. Lutz

"While I was traveling on the way to Cupertino, a long trip because of the plane connection, I had the chance of reading your book through which I had the fortune of understanding the strength that exists within the Jewish people and that unites you: it all begins in the family bond. I truly found it very interesting; I wish all families could have the luck of keeping their members together in such a way. I hope my children read this book that I enjoyed so much. I was also very interested by the way that you portrayed the fact that all throughout your life you had ups and downs in your business, nevertheless, thanks to that union and the personal efforts made by each one, you have made things change and have become the successful entrepreneurs you are now."

Gare Fabils de Zaldo

"With great pleasure I received the volume you wrote about your father. Ari, I thank you sincerely for such an interesting gift."

Jorge Tamayo

"First of all, I want to thank you for the time you dedicated us on our visit to Mexico this last week. As you already know, I am extremely fond of you all; I spent my entire flight back home reading the book about your daddy. It was magnificent. I loved it, and to tell you the truth, there were numerous times that I felt my eyes fill with tears."

Fred V. Luss

"With all appropriateness I received that beautiful monument to the model filial love that you dedicated to the memory of your father, my dear friend Wulf, 'Adolfito', as he let me call him personally.

I express to you my gratitude for sending me this moving piece of work and I can only tell you that he must have felt very satisfied about having formed a family as admirable as yours."

Agustín Arriaga Rivera

"Thank you so much for honoring me when we said farewell at the end of the Hebrew University breakfast reunion by giving me a copy of the book *my Father*, dedicated to the memory of your father, Wulf Kahan.

I can't do other than offer you the most affectionate hug and the most effusive congratulations, feeling that my eyes start to shed tears of emotion as I do so, for you managed to materialize an idea that many of us could have thought of, but it is very few who can actually crystallize it and have it done in such a brief period of time."

Enrique Grunstein

"I have read the book attentively and through its pages I have been able to confirm once more that people with principles such as yours do not exist only by chance; they are always the result of a firm upbringing like the one you received from your father.

Many anecdotes, many experiences; all of them full of enriching concepts.

Lives like the one Wulf Kahan led are worthy of being reviewed.

I would like to repeat that 'the greatest satisfaction that a son could ever have is having responsible parents who are loved by the society they live in; knowing the devotion and affection they have for each one of their children, and see the flame of love between them is still alive.' I profoundly share this thought which identifies me with you and, once more, makes me admire your way of thinking and living as an honorable man, concerned about the well-being of his family and all the people around you."

Enrique Bustamante Martínez

"I didn't send you this letter until now because, as I have already told you, I wanted to read the book about your father before writing back.

Just as I suspected, although the book is based mostly on your father, Wulf Kahan, it clearly portrays the history of hard work and dedication in all the Kahan family during so, so many years. I was moved when I read how your grandmother, despite all the work that meant keeping that house in order, would still find the time to feed and take care of so many dogs in the neighborhood where she lived."

Guillermo A. Grimm

"It is a book so full of humaneness and so interesting, that I was able to read it all in one day; I didn't want to stop in the middle of it."

Gastón Cantarell

"Being under the instructions of the Israeli Ambassador in Mexico, Mr. David Tourgeman, I congratulate you on your interesting and humane book titled my Father, which shows not only aspects of family relationships, but also includes an outline of the life of the Jewish people in Mexico, clearly appreciated throughout your narration."

Silvia L. Saad

"From beginning to end, I read the book; tribute that you fondly compiled and had printed in memory of your beloved father, Don Wulf. Very few sons can have the great satisfaction, dear Ari, of taking the time and work to accomplish this magnificent compilation of so many interviews."

Juan Horn Reyes

"I have read your book with great pleasure and even re-read some chapters and thoughts about DON ADOLFO or DON WULF (yes, with capital letters) expressed by his great-grandchildren, children, sons and daughters-in-law, friends, and collaborators. What a unique man! What an AMAZING FELLOW!

...All of the chapter titled 'The Waiting' is beautiful, yet shocking: beautiful for the love and support everyone gave him; touching and shocking for finding that a handsome, strong, loved man went through a terrible physical (but not spiritual) collapse in the last years of his existence...

Ari, both our fathers' lives had a lot in common: they were both true fanatics and faithful believers if friendship; they had the pleasure of knowing how to give, rather than to receive; they were extremely proud of their humble origins, which they not only did not hide, but they even showed off; both inseparable companions to their wives, who they loved and respected all their lives; lovers of beautiful things, they enjoyed them and, above all, they liked sharing them; generous hosts sharing their tables; both presumptuous about their strong legs, they loved others to feel how hard they got when they squeezed their muscles. So many things that identified them, Ari, that for a moment I thought I was reading about my father."

Alberto Bello López

"Today I am sitting at my desk; I swivel my chair around and lean back on it. I turn to the window and I find myself staring outside. With the corner of my eye, I catch a glimpse of the book I found when I arrived here this morning. You know what book it is that I'm referring to.

Frankly, I opened it without much interest. I threw a look at one of its lines as if I were rolling a pair of dice on the page.

I was captivated. I decided it was about time that I treat myself to a half an hour of spare time. One hour has gone by and I am about to finish reading the book. Realizing this, I decided to steal a moment of your time to tell you about my joy. If I had to give a title to these paragraphs it would be 'A Friend On My Desk'.

The book starts talking about the tough times. That alone gave me some strength. From that moment on I just glided through the text. I found a shelter, I remembered, I meditated. The most important thing about it was not the strength it took for him to work, but rather to understand what he worked for. Thank you.

You know? I'm going to call my father and invite him out to lunch."

Victor O'Farrill T.

"As soon as I had the book in my hands I started reading it and I finished that same day. I lived some of the things narrated there; I found out about others through the same people that tell them in the book; and some others I simply had no idea about.

When I accompanied you and your family to the cemetery, I trembled with emotion as I confirmed that in spite of having been the Boss, he had also been a dear friend to many. Maybe he could have lived many more years in g od health and happiness, I thought, and as I stood there, overwhelmed, with my head down, I started comparing him to a large and strong tree that had not been able to make it through the storm; and then I cried and remembered something I once read that was very beautiful, and I related that thought with him:

'Strength and fighting always go together. The greatest reward that can come of fighting is strength. Life is a battle and the greatest joy is conquering it. When a man is in pursuit of things that are easy to obtain, he becomes weak.' But your father was always a very strong man."

Gloria Morales

"It is our wish to express our deepest gratitude for the book you kindly sent us to be kept at the library of the *Colegio Israelita de México*[42].

...Many of our alumni have come back to our school as parents; they have brought their children to us, and have showed concern for the well-being of our institution. Some others have returned to us as professionals and have become a part of our teaching staff for the generations that followed theirs' and thus, they have carried out the dreams of the institution's founders. Others remember it fondly and come back to school with their hearts and their feelings. This is the way you have done it: through your dedication in your book and through the concern you show for today's young people who are getting an education at the *Colegio Israelita de México*."

Jaime Edelson and Raquel Kleimberg

"The automotive industry in Mexico has a history that cannot do without Wulf Kahan and his enterprise, or better said, his family enterprise, because the group that form the Kahan companies of yesterday and today has been a family community whose members have agreed all the time on one common economic objective, ever since Mexico still lacked the industrial aspirations that were then concentrated in the cities of Monterrey and Puebla.

...When Don Adolfo passed away in 1992, he left the company Kahan Automotriz established for his descendants' benefit, and thanks to which the popular use of the automobile in Mexico has expanded a great deal. An enterprise such as this is a model for the crucial

[42] *Israelite School of Mexico.*

phase that our country is in, when we must decide what development prototype to take."

Gastón Pardo

"As I skimmed through the pages of the book I realized its value as a human testimony... I cordially congratulate you on your filial love that has led you to disclose the human qualities and virtues your father possessed; something that has honored you greatly."

Jorge Planas

"The book you published in homage to your father's life, rather than to his memory, moved us deeply; not only because of its humane and affectionate contents, but also for the fact that you dedicated yourself to its creation, and for the profound meaning of this accomplishment.

If all the things this book narrates were not enough to establish the magnitude of your father's personality, along with the role and the personality of your mother -undoubtedly, a fundamental part of his life- it would then be enough to know that they had a son like yourself, and that they inspired in him the qualities that make us proud to count you among the people we love most, in order to celebrate the importance of his example."

Georges and Ariel

"I thank you endlessly for the book about your beloved father's life, which I consider simply exemplary. Also, my heartfelt congratulations on having made this biography possible."

Nicolás Zapata

"I thank you very much, Ari, for the present featuring that very humane information written from the heart: the book you created about your dear father. I truly loved it."

Chilpa

"I have finished reading your book *my Father*, regarding the life and work of your distinguished father. I would like to comment on an aspect in your book that truly amazed me: I'm referring to the narration made by his friends. Our wise men taught us '*tov shem tov*' (it is good to have a good name)."

Rabbi Y. Rubinstein

"A peaceful and inspiring Shabbat is coming to an end; one that I spent in my office, rearranging some papers and continuing my reading of the beautiful book my Father, which I thank you for from the bottom of my heart. I have passed the chapter about the Family and I feel as if I knew all of you already... And how many anecdotes and events remind me of my own parents and family!

I hope to finish reading this book tonight and I'm sure that, as it happens with certain exquisite musical masterpieces, I'll come back to read this endless proof of love and unity of a great Jewish family for a second time."

Roger Berensohn

"When Wulf Kahan passed away, it was Rabbi Rittner who dedicated the last words of farewell to his memory: 'Do not ask how he died, but rather how he lived; not what was his position, but rather try to know if he was a sensitive man; not what were his beliefs or which was his sanctuary, but rather how did he help the ones who needed it; not try reading information in the papers about his passing, but rather ask how many people grieve his death.'

A fulminating balance yet, without a doubt, just! Of course, justice is quite uncomfortable for some. We must say that Adolfo Kahan lived to do humanity good; he was a sensitive man, respectful of the Virgin of Guadalupe, located up to this day on 23 Mina Street, without being a Catholic, relevant proof of how his beliefs or his sanctuary did not represent an obstacle for him to do others good."

Fernando Mota Martínez

"We write to you, Your Excellency, the President of the United States of America, Mr. William Clinton, on behalf of the Mexican Front for Human Rights, institution which I have the honor to preside, to express to you our knowledge that one of the main concerns of your government's policies is reviewing the strategy to reactivate the United States economy...it is necessary to reactivate the economy of all developing countries.

...It is likewise necessary to change the management policies so the workers -the main partners in all companies- obtain proper profit sharing in their enterprises.

Wulf Kahan, one of the most important entrepreneurs in Mexico and Latin America, established the following bases: the well-being of the workers must be one of the main concerns for all entrepreneurs; the client must always be satisfied; both workers and bosses must go to the aid of any fellow worker anguished in case of an emergency; two thirds of the company's earnings must be destined for salaries and expenses, while the remaining third must go to the company; one must select, train, and protect one's staff; it is necessary to spend time with the workers, visit them at home; every member of the staff must own a car and, in order to achieve this, they must be granted extensive credit terms.

...Wulf Kahan established a flourishing enterprise called *Kahan Automotriz, S.A. de C.V.* The automotive production in the United States has a very broad market thanks to this type of companies; that is why it is of such importance to seriously consider the example described above. This type of enterprises are important factors for the reactivation of both the American and Mexican economies."

Benjamín Laureano Luna

"After having read *my Father*, I confirm that from a crystalline spring only pure water can flow. With elegant simpleness you describe Mr. Wulf's profound philosophy and you show us is path of love, work, effort, and faith in life. It is a lesson we all must learn, especially all statesmen, businessmen, parents, teachers, government officials, and whoever feels a responsibility towards all humanity.

Your father's life is an example of great principles and in your lines you shows us, in a very sensitive manner, that it was strengthened intensely by the vision, loyalty, self-assurance, encouragement, and care of Doña Estela, his companion: with no doubt, this is a double blessing for all of you.

During this particularly difficult year, reading the story of the man who loved Mexico and believed in it despite its vicissitudes, has fortified my convictions and renewed my hopes."

Raul Muñoz Astrudillo

"I have read a considerable number of biographies about all kinds of personalities, but never had I been so moved as much as I was with the one that narrates the life of Wulf Kahan. Knowing him makes you have the desire of trying to rival your own courage to face destiny and live it.

It is a book worthy of being read and having it as bedside book because or its strengthening message."

Mario A. Ortega

"Ari, despite of me not having had the pleasure of meeting your father, thanks to your efforts to compile so many testimonies, I have the feeling that he was a human being in the highest sense of the word.

Your book made me remember my father who, like yours, was an immigrant and loved Mexico dearly. He fought for his country and, most of all, he formed a united family to which he taught the same principles: hard work, honesty, helping others, and love for our nation. I found it very touching to read through these pages."

Julio Zamora Bátiz

"I find in the book some very interesting ideas, applicable to the life of any human being who has any desire of improving him or herself."

Jaime del Valle Noriega

"I fully agree with you, Ari: 'Death can put an end to life, but never will it end a relationship.' Enclosed I send you a copy of the speech my father wrote and read at his 100th birthday party. I'm sure that both you and I feel very proud of their memory."

Simón Rubinstein

"I thank you endlessly, Ari, for the opportunity you gave me of reading a testimony of courage and good living.

Us parents wish that our children outshine us in everything they do and by this, have the greatest of satisfactions and have in their future the best encounter with Our Eternal Father, when their time comes.

Ari, we admire your behavior as an honorable son to a unique father. The messages and experiences of countless friends have let us one more character, someone that in our memories was always a fighter.

I feel identified with many aspects of his fruitful life: his constant restlessness, his desire for accomplishing many things, his indomitable spirit, and his deep love for his family, looking out for its perfection, even if he had to be strict for that to happen.

Near the end of his life he wished to transcend to a full existence in eternity, for us believers know that our life is only a waiting room before we have the opportunity of enjoying our Creator.

We are with you in your prayers and the ones of multitudes of admirers and people who are grateful for the courtesies and actions carried out by your father."

Blanca and Antonio Fernández

"Thank you, Ari. Thanks very much for giving me so many beautiful things in your book, *my Father*.

I have just read the third edition and you took me by the hand, as if through a time tunnel, back to my own life; to travel through happy passages of our life, of the life that mom and dad gave us with so much wisdom and love.

For me, your book has been an oasis of peace, a place

in which I can look for shelter whenever I am feeling sad and where I can find the light to take decisions when I feel the most confused.

Unfortunately, the passing of time and the daily routine start erasing the memories of beautiful images, like daddy's smile, his simpleness in the knowledge of life, and the strong, yet feminine figure of mom always ready for any battle, always alking on dad's right side. Your book rekindles those moments and dad is still alive in each one of your letters.

Ari, as I read what his grandchildren and great-grandchildren wrote, it was like going against the laws of life, thinking how little time they had to enjoy him, but your book is going to help those new generations to still keep enjoying his presence.

Dear brother, even though it is plagiarism, I agree with you on the fact that if it were possible to choose parenthood, I would have chosen Estela and Adolfo Kahan's parenthood."

Ruth Kahan de Gancz

"There is always a silver lining to every cloud, Ari. When my wife fell ill, She had to set a limit to all her restlessness and treated herself to the pleasure of reading your book and, at the same time, made me become very fond of it.

What a man! And what a great book you created!

I now have the desire of writing my father's life. There is so much richness in these, the lives of our elders! You could never imagine how much I think of you and your community, the committed Jewish people, whenever I read The Old Testament during mass, and just how much I wish to tell you about the good things in what we call The New Testament.

Knowing the chilling events that our dear nation is facing, I think that, above all, we must stick together and make sure that the human principles prevail and spread among the world population."

Agustín Escobar Lafarga

"I have thought a lot about the great knowledge of life that you possess, Ari. The advice that flows from the pages of your book has helped me greatly, and with it I have managed to focus better on my objectives."

Eduardo Blocker

"The sorrow that came with the loss of our son[43] is now easier to tolerate for your laudatory concepts praise a memory dear to us, and the words of *my Father*. The book ou kindly sent us, as well as the comfort that came from reading it, has helped us bear the pain of his absence."

Luis Colosio Fernández

[43] *Luis Donaldo Colosio, presidential candidate for the PRI, assassinated on March 23rd, 1994.*